126296

The BHS
Training Ma
FOR
Stage 3

The BHS
Training Manual
FOR
Stage 3

The British Horse Society
Registered Charity No. 210504

Islay Auty FBHS

KENILWORTH PRESS

First published in 2005 by
Kenilworth Press Ltd
Addington
Buckingham
MK18 2JR

British Library Cataloguing in Publication Data
A catalogue record for this book is available from the British Library.

ISBN 0-872119-83-2

Layout by Kenilworth Press
Line drawings by Dianne Breeze and Carole Vincer
Line diagrams by Michael J. Stevens

Printed in Great Britain by MPG Books Ltd (www.mpg-books.co.uk)

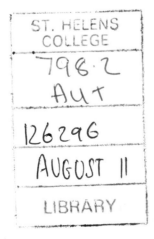

Contents

Picture Acknowledgements

All line drawings are by **Dianne Breeze**, with the exception of those on pages 44, 45, 46, 51, 52 and 53, which are by **Carole Vincer**.

The jumping diagrams are by **Michael J. Stevens**

Picture sources
The author and publishers wish to acknowledge the following books as sources for some of the illustrations:

- **The BHS Manual of Equitation**, Consultant Editor Islay Auty FBHS, published by Kenilworth Press

- **The BHS Complete Manual of Stable Management,** Consultant Editor Islay Auty FBHS, published by Kenilworth Press

- **No Foot, No Horse**, by Gail Williams and Martin Deacon, published by Kenilworth Press

- **Threshold Picture Guide No. 16, Feet and Shoes**, by Toni Webber, published by Kenilworth Press

- **Threshold Picture Guide No. 43, Functional Anatomy**, by Dr Chris Colles BVetMed, PhD, MRCVS, published by Kenilworth Press

- **The Examinations Handbook**, published by the British Horse Society

How to Use This Book

The aim of this book is to provide students working towards Stage 3 with detailed guidance on how to prepare thoroughly for the examination. Similarly to the other books in this series, the information is set out in two sections: Horse Knowledge and Care, and Riding – reflecting the two parts of the Stage 3 exam. Each of the two sections of the exam can be taken separately on different occasions, or they can be tackled together on the same examination day. If you pass the Horse Knowledge and Care section you will be given the BHS Groom's Certificate, which indicates that you are competent to care for a number of horses and ponies (up to four) with less supervision than a person of Stage 2 ability. The attainment of the Riding section, together with the Horse Knowledge and Care section, gives you the full Stage 3 certificate.

You will find that the book follows a clear pattern. The syllabus is divided into **elements** under general headings (e.g. clothing, saddlery, etc.). Under the list of elements there is information on '**What the examiner is looking for**', which is followed by advice on '**How to become competent**'. The book will direct you to where to find information and practical experience.

There are no short cuts to achieving practical competence. 'Practice makes perfect' may be an old saying but it still holds good today. Your past experience with horses, which should already be providing you with a sound foundation of practical competence, will be tested more searchingly at this level. And your practical ability to 'read' horses and be aware of how best to handle or ride them will be challenged a little more pointedly. The book should enable you to build both ability and confidence, giving you a very clear, structured reference to your progress towards attempting and achieving the required standard.

Understanding the Stage 3 Exam

After Stage 2

After your success in passing Stage 2 the sensible route is confidently to consolidate your knowledge before you start to think about Stage 3. Unless you have come to BHS exams a little later in life and therefore have a wealth of practical hands-on experience with horses, which can help you to 'fast track' the exams, do not aim for Stage 3 too soon after passing Stage 2. Just as after taking GCSE exams it takes another training commitment to aim for 'A' levels, so it is with Stage 2 and Stage 3. No two people are the same, and it is therefore pointless to give an optimum length of study time between Stages 2 and 3. Suffice it to say that at Stage 3 the standard of both the riding and the stable management are considerably more challenging than at Stage 2.

Give yourself time and plenty of opportunity to ride many different horses, and be conscientious in your approach to good yard work and horse management. Good handling of horses with practical, efficient fitting of a wide range of equipment, backed up by sound theoretical knowledge is expected of a good Stage 3 candidate. The Stage 3 rider must be competent and confident to ride horses on the flat and over fences (show jumps and cross-country). You must be able to maintain the level of the horse's work and show ability to ride and lunge horses that may be fit and in competition work. You must be able to work horses correctly and also talk about their way of going.

Examination format

As mentioned, the two sections of the exam can be taken on different days or both on the same day.

The Horse Knowledge and Care section

This section of the exam involves a **theory session** in a class room, with discussion on such subjects as fitness, feeding and care of the horse at grass. A **practical session** will involve assessing a horse's action when he is trotted up in hand, loading for travel, and fitting equipment for competition, including exercise bandages. You will also be required to lunge a horse for exercise. A **practical oral session** will cover the horse's physiology with regard to respiration and circulation, the superficial muscles, sites of wear and tear, and 'lumps and bumps' (e.g. splints, windgalls and curbs). During all the stable management sections you will be part of a group of up to five, with one examiner per section.

The Riding section

The riding section will involve a session **on the flat** where you will ride two or three horses. Each horse will be in a snaffle bridle and usually a dressage saddle, although some horses may wear general-purpose saddles. After you have ridden one (or possibly more) of the horses, you will be asked to talk to the examiner about how you found the horse. The riding section on the flat lasts around 50–60 minutes, and there will be a group of up to five of you riding at the same time, usually in an indoor school.

The ridden section also involves riding a horse over show jumps and taking another over a number of cross-country fences (six to ten). The **show jumping** will start with a progressive warm-up, developing over a grid, building from one to three fences. Then the grid will lead into or be incorporated in a course of fences which you must ride in good style and balance. The **cross-country** will be on a different horse to the one you have show jumped. You will have ample opportunity at the beginning of the day to walk the show-jumping and the cross-country courses. This opportunity should not be missed as it essential to know exactly where you will be riding and what you will be jumping.

In all sections of the Stage 3 exam you should be demonstrating competence and show a degree of confidence and self-belief. The examiner should feel confident that he or she could leave you to exercise a sensible but fit horse, either on the flat, jumping or on the lunge, and that you could look after this horse (and up to three more) capably and with minimal supervision, on a day-to-day basis.

Stage 3 and the PTT

Remember that achieving the Stage 3 exam (Riding and Horse Knowledge and Care) gives you half of the requirement for the BHS Assistant Instructor's certificate. Passing the Preliminary Teaching Test and then fulfilling 500 hours' teaching practice will give you the mandatory requirement for the award of the British Horse Society Assistant Instructor's certificate.

Stage 3
Horse Knowledge and Care

Syllabus

Candidates must be physically fit in order to carry out yard and fieldwork efficiently, without undue stress and strain. They will be expected to demonstrate competent use of time.

Candidates will be expected to give practical demonstrations as well as be involved in discussion of selected tasks and topics. All work required for Stage 2 should be carried out to an even higher standard of efficiency, and candidates should show a responsible attitude.

General: An increase of responsibility; looking after a number of horses and ponies (up to four) with less supervision; ensuring that horses, stables, yards and fields are safe and in good order.

IMPORTANT: Candidates are advised to check that they are working from the latest examination syllabus, as examination content and procedure are liable to alteration. Contact the BHS Examinations Office for up-to-date information regarding the syllabus.

British Horse Society – Stage 3 Syllabus

Stage 3 – Horse Knowledge and Care
Candidates must be physically fit in order to carry out yard and fieldwork efficiently without undue stress and strain. They will be expected to demonstrate competent use of time. Candidates will be expected to give practical demonstrations as well as be involved in discussion of selected tasks and topics. All work required for Stage 2 should be carried out to an even higher standard of efficiency and candidates should show a responsible attitude.

General – An increase of responsibility; looking after a number of horses and ponies (up to 4) with less supervision; ensuring that horses, stables, yard and fields are safe and in good order.

Unit code number S3CARE			
Learning Outcomes	**Element**	**Assessment Criteria**	
The candidate should be able to:		The candidate has achieved this outcome because s/he can:	**Influence**
Clothing Put on exercise/schooling bandages, and know their benefits and disadvantages.	1.1.1	Demonstrate correct application and securing of exercise and/or schooling bandages	Compulsory
	1.1.2	Explain the consequences of poor application of exercise and schooling bandages	Supporting
	1.1.3	Give examples of suitable materials to use for protection under bandages	Supporting
Saddlery Know the correct principles and fitting of saddlery and bits in general use, including those used for training and competition work.	2.1.1	Demonstrate correct application and fitting of tack commonly used in dressage competitions	Compulsory
	2.1.2	Demonstrate correct application and fitting of tack commonly used in cross-country competitions	Compulsory
	2.2.1	Explain indications of incorrect fitting and/or inappropriate saddlery, and the possible consequences	Supporting
	2.3.1	Explain the action of a variety of bits in general use	Compulsory
	2.4.1	Apply and fit a variety of boots used for protection, suitable for various competitions	Compulsory
Know how to organise a saddle room and its contents.	2.5.1	Describe the perfect tack-room	Supporting
Know how to clean and store saddlery and rugs.	2.6.1	Give examples of appropriate practice for storing tack and rugs	Supporting
Travelling Horses Know the procedures when travelling horses by trailer or horse box and safe procedures for loading and unloading.	3.1.1	Carry out appropriate checks on transport vehicles to ensure the horses' safety and well-being during loading and transportation, and report any discrepancies	Compulsory
	3.2.1	Carry out checks on the loading horses' clothing and report on its suitability	Compulsory
	3.3.1	List equipment to be taken (water etc.)	Supporting
	3.4.1	Explain to an assistant the loading procedure with regard to the safety of yourself, the horse and others	Supporting
	3.4.2	Explain to an assistant the unloading procedure with regard to the safety of yourself, the horse and others	Supporting
	3.5.1	Give examples of procedures for loading difficult horses with regard to the safety of yourself, the horse and others	Supporting
	3.6.1	Demonstrate how to safely load and secure a horse	Compulsory
	3.6.2	Demonstrate how to safely unload a horse	Compulsory
Lungeing Lunge an experienced fit horse efficiently in an enclosed space.	4.1.1	Use lunge equipment safely and to good effect	Compulsory
	4.2.1	Show a safe appropriate lunge technique for an unknown horse	Compulsory
	4.3.1	Use exercises suitable for developing and maintaining control whilst exercising the horse	Compulsory
	4.3.2	Demonstrate an appropriate method of exercise, showing appreciation for the horse's balance and fitness level	Compulsory
	4.4.1	Demonstrate an understanding of the importance of rhythm and balance	Supporting
	4.5.1	Explain the value of lungeing	Supporting
	4.6.1	Describe the tack and facilities required	Supporting

Unit code number S3CARE			
Learning Outcomes	Element	Assessment Criteria	Influence
The candidate should be able to:		The candidate has achieved this outcome because s/he can:	
Stable Design	5.1.1	Describe the perfect stable yard	Compulsory
	5.2.1	Give examples of good ventilation systems	Compulsory
	5.2.2	Give examples of good drainage systems	Compulsory
Understand simple planning of the stable yard and the advantages and disadvantages of different types of stabling and fittings.	5.3.1	Outline the advantages and disadvantages of keeping horses in a traditional stable yard	Supporting
	5.3.2	Outline the advantages and disadvantages of keeping horses in an American barn-style stable yard	Supporting
	5.4.1	Give the advantages and disadvantages of prefabricated wooden stables	Supporting
	5.5.1	Identify areas of importance when allocating stabling to specific horses	Compulsory
	5.6.1	Give examples of labour-saving stable fittings/devices	Supporting
Anatomy and Physiology	6.1.1	Discuss a presented horse's general proportions with regard to conformation	Supporting
Know basic good and bad conformation.	6.1.2	Discuss normal and abnormal forelimb conformation	Supporting
	6.1.3	Discuss normal and abnormal hind limb conformation	Supporting
	6.1.4	Discuss how the presented horse's conformation may affect his way of going	Supporting
	6.2.1	Show and name the horse's main superficial muscles	Supporting
Know the horse's main trunk muscles used to move his limbs and to support and carry his rider.	6.3.1	Name the tendons in a forelimb	Compulsory
	6.3.2	Show where the individual tendons run.	Supporting
	6.4.1	Name the ligaments found in a forelimb	Compulsory
	6.4.2	Show where the individual ligaments are	Supporting
Know the basic structure of the leg below the knee/hock.	6.5.1	Identify the sesamoid bones and describe their function	Supporting
	6.6.1	Designate the respiratory tract and/or the basic function of each section	Supporting
	6.6.2	Identify a horse's respiration rate	Compulsory
	6.6.3	Describe the symptoms of respiratory problems in the horse	Compulsory
	6.7.1	Give a basic description of the function of the main parts of the circulatory system	Supporting
	6.7.2	Explain the functions of the circulatory system	Compulsory
Know the basic outline of the horse's respiratory and circulatory systems.	6.7.3	Explain how the heart rate can be a fitness indicator	Supporting
	6.7.4	Give examples of dealing with circulatory problems such as arterial bleeding from a wound and filled legs	Compulsory
	6.8.1	Identify and/or designate bony enlargements such as splints	Compulsory
	6.8.2	Identify and/ or designate bursal enlargements on the horse's limbs	Compulsory
Recognise basic causes of lameness and know their treatments.	6.8.3	Name and give the causes, symptoms and treatments of bursal enlargements, tendon and ligament strains and bony enlargements found in the horse's lower limb	Compulsory
The Horse's Foot	7.1.1	Identify good/poor aspects of the balance of a horse's front feet	Compulsory
Understand good foot conformation and the effects of poor hoof balance.	7.2.1	Describe and show a horse's hoof-pastern axis	Supporting
	7.2.2	Describe the possible problems caused by an incorrect hoof-pastern axis.	Supporting
	7.3.1	Identify indications of the horse's health and way of going by the state of wear of his shoes.	Supporting

Unit code number S3CARE			
Learning Outcomes	**Element**	**Assessment Criteria**	**Influence**
The candidate should be able to:		The candidate has achieved this outcome because s/he can:	
Shoeing	8.1.1	Describe the characteristics of a well-shod foot	Compulsory
	8.2.1	Explain the purpose of a variety of shoes including hunter shoes, rolled toes, feather-edged, wide web shoes	Supporting
Know what to look for in a well-shod foot. Special shoes for special cases. Use of foot-pads and studs. Recognise faulty shoeing and know the consequent ill-effects.	8.3.1	Give examples of what you would not wish to see in a newly shod foot and why	Compulsory
	8.4.1	Give examples of when to use pads	Supporting
	8.5.1	Describe where to fit studs and how you keep stud holes in good order	Compulsory
	8.5.2	Give examples of appropriate studs for a variety of ground conditions.	Supporting
Action	9.1.1	Describe to an assistant the 'trotting up' procedure.	Supporting
	9.1.2	Demonstrate how to 'trot a horse up'	Compulsory
Know the sequence of the horse's footfalls at all gaits; good and faulty action.	9.2.1	Identify basic qualities and faults in movement using correct terminology	Supporting
	9.3.1	Describe the horse's posture and action when lame on a forelimb	Compulsory
Identify foreleg/hind limb lameness.	9.3.2	Describe the horse's posture and action when lame on a hind limb	Compulsory
Horse Behaviour	10.1.1	Give examples of aspects of equine conduct/maturity that make it unwise to run particular horses with a herd	Compulsory
Know how to deal with young, highly spirited or problem horses, including those with stable vices.	10.2.1	Explain behaviour and practices designed to gain the horse's confidence in stables	Supporting
	10.3.1	Give examples of stable vices, their consequences and ways of controlling them	Compulsory
	10.4.1	Give examples of how discomfort and/or undue stress are shown in the ridden horse's behaviour.	Supporting
Horse Health	11.1.1	List the contents of a well-stocked first-aid cabinet for horses	Compulsory
Knowledge of treating minor injuries, minor ailments, sickness and lameness; how to prevent them and when to call the veterinary surgeon and what information to give.	11.2.1	Explain cold hosing and the problems you may use it for	Compulsory
	11.2.2	Explain tubbing and the problems you may use it for	Supporting
	11.2.3	Explain poulticing/hot fomentations and the problems you may use them for	Supporting
	11.3.1	Give the causes, symptoms and treatment of colic	Compulsory
	11.3.2	Give the causes, symptoms and treatment of azoturia	Supporting
	11.3.3	Give the causes, symptoms and treatment of laminitis	Supporting
Know how to administer medicine and implement worming procedures.	11.4.1	Give the principles of sick nursing	Compulsory
	11.4.2	Explain an isolation procedure and the diseases you might use it for	Compulsory
	11.5.1	Describe a suitable worming routine	Compulsory
Fittening	12.1.1	Give a suitable period of time for getting a horse fit for Pony Club one-day event or Riding Club one day event	Compulsory
	12.1.2	Describe suitable work given during the first 3–4 weeks of an appropriate fittening programme for Pony Club or Riding Club events	Supporting
Know procedures for preparing and looking after fit horses and how to prepare horses for the show ring and other competitions.	12.1.3	Describe suitable work given during the second 3–4 weeks of an appropriate fittening programme for Pony Club or Riding Club events	Compulsory
	12.1.4	Describe suitable work given during the third 3–4 weeks of an appropriate fittening programme for Pony Club or Riding Club events	Compulsory
	12.2.1	Explain the value of using walking exercise, hills, trot and canter work, short gallops, lungeing	Compulsory
	12.3.1	Explain how a fittening program may differ for 'show' horses	Supporting
	12.4.1	Give examples of a routine week that is appropriate for maintaining a horse's fitness level	Supporting

Unit code number S3CARE			
Learning Outcomes	**Element**	**Assessment Criteria**	**Influence**
The candidate should be able to:		The candidate has achieved this outcome because s/he can:	
General Knowledge Know the risks and responsibilities involved when riding on the public highway. Correct procedures in the event of accidents. Safety rules and fire precautions in the stable yard. Know about the BHS and its departments.	13.1.1	Describe correct procedures when riding in a group on the highway	Compulsory
	13.1.2	Give examples of correct leading in hand on the road	Compulsory
	13.2.1	Explain the procedure to be adopted in the event of a fire in stables	Compulsory
	13.3.1	Explain what is meant by the term 'risk assessment', and give an example	Supporting
	13.4.1	Give examples of the responsibilities of individual BHS departments	Supporting
	13.4.2	List the benefits of being a BHS member	Compulsory
	13.5.1	Describe the action to be taken in the event of an accident involving a rider	Compulsory
Grassland Care Know the basic management required to maintain grazing paddocks in suitable condition for horses/ponies living out or on daily turn out.	14.1.1	Explain the reasons for harrowing pasture	Supporting
	14.1.2	Explain the reasons for rolling pasture	Supporting
	14.1.3	Explain the reasons for fertilising and topping paddocks	Supporting
	14.1.4	Outline a pasture maintenance regime	Supporting
	14.2.1	Explain the benefits of grazing horse pasture with sheep and/or cattle	Compulsory
	14.3.1	Give minimum acreage ratios required for horses	Compulsory
Watering and Feeding Understand the value of grass and concentrates and the significance of carbohydrates, proteins, fats and oils, minerals, vitamins, fibre and water in the horse's diet. Ability to monitor and organise the feed store.	15.1.1	Explain why water is vital to the horse	Compulsory
	15.2.1	Describe the importance of carbohydrates in the horse's diet	Supporting
	15.2.2	Describe the importance of protein in the horse's diet	Supporting
	15.2.3	Describe the importance of fats and oils in the horse's diet	Supporting
	15.2.4	Describe the importance of minerals and vitamins in the horse's diet	Supporting
	15.2.5	Explain why fibre is so important in the horse's diet	Compulsory
	15.2.6	Discuss the meaning of the phrase 'balanced diet' and give an example of a balanced diet for specific types of horse/pony	Compulsory
	15.3.1	Give examples and underlying reasons for adjusting the grass kept pony/horse's diet through the seasons.	Compulsory
	15.4.1	Give examples of quantities of bulk to concentrate ratios for maintenance and for horses in light and medium work	Compulsory
	15.5.1	Explain how to monitor and arrange/store feed stocks	Supporting

For those of you who have not seen the syllabus in this format before (it was revised in 2004), a little explanation will reassure you that the standards and requirements of the Stage 3 exam are unchanged. The syllabus is clearly divided into Elements broadly covering individual topics (e.g. clothing, saddlery), and sections within each element break down the expected knowledge and understanding. Within this book the following symbols are used:

C = COMPULSORY

S = SUPPORTING

Compulsory elements appear in the practical and theoretical parts of your exam. It is likely that most, if not all, of the compulsory elements will be examined during your Stage 3. As the name suggests, the supporting elements add depth and weight to the demonstration of competence that should be shown in the compulsory elements.

Make sure that you are competent and confident in all areas of the compulsory requirements. Make sure that you feel comfortable with all the supporting elements – there should be nothing within the syllabus that you have never heard of!

Remember that **all** work that was required in Stages 1 and 2 should now be more assured and carried out with greater confidence and to a higher level of efficiency. Candidates should show an increasing awareness of the needs of the horse(s) in their care. They must also show an understanding of the importance of co-operating and communicating with fellow workers. In addition, candidates will be expected to show knowledge and practical ability in the subjects that follow.

Clothing

Put on exercise/schooling bandages and know their benefits and disadvantages.

ELEMENT

C   **1.1.1** Demonstrate correct application and securing of exercise and/or schooling bandages.

S   **1.1.2** Explain the consequences of poor application of exercise and schooling bandages.

S   **1.1.3** Give examples of suitable materials to use for protection under bandages.

What the examiner is looking for

- You are likely to be asked to apply one or two exercise bandages (or bandages in which the horse could be expected to work/exercise). (Element 1.1.1)

- There are many types of bandage on the market these days. Many dressage riders prefer to school horses in inelastic bandages. These are made of a fleece-like material which cannot be applied too tightly, and therefore they are frequently applied without any 'padding' or additional material underneath.

- 'Exercise' bandages are still the choice of some riders for event and jumping horses, and these are usually applied with some type of under-material applied to the leg first. These bandages are generally made of an elastic stretchy type of fabric. Gamgee tissue is still referred to but is well outdated nowadays by such custom-made products as 'Fybagee'. (Element 1.1.3)

- The choice of which padding to use under bandages is dictated by personal preference, cost, and the bulk of the layer beneath the bandage. It is also possible to use a type of polystyrene shell (Porter boots) which are shaped to the leg and designed specifically for use under elastic bandages.

- The primary concern is that the under layer provides a smooth, even contact around the leg, onto which the bandage is applied. Natural fibre materials prevent a tendency for the leg to sweat.

- Bandages must be applied with firm, even pressure, and with no increase in pressure when the tapes or Velcro strips are secured to keep the bandage in place. (Element 1.1.1)

- Poorly applied bandages can be extremely dangerous. There is a risk of a bandage coming loose and tripping the horse up; and if overtight could cause damage to the tissues. (Element 1.1.2)

- You must demonstrate competence and efficiency in applying exercise bandages, completing the task at an appropriate speed.

- You should always show an awareness of your own position in relation to that of the horse in the stable, especially when applying hind leg bandages. (For example, do not position yourself in a tight space between the wall and the horse's hind leg.)

How to become competent

- Exercise bandages are not used extensively these days because of the wide range of alternative leg protection that is available on the market. Because bandaging is 'examined' as a task in the Stage 3, it is essential that you have practised sufficiently to ensure that you are competent and can apply bandages to all four legs in an efficient way.

- If you do not have a horse that is regularly wearing bandages for work, then apply bandages as often as you can (preferably every day for at least a month before your exam).

- Ask someone with greater experience than yourself to check the bandages.

- Look at horses in competition and notice what they are wearing on their legs. If you have the opportunity, watch competition riders applying bandages and notice how firmly they fit them and what padding (if any) they use underneath.

- Seek the opinion of riders, instructors and your vet for their thoughts on the pros and cons of bandaging.

- At some stage in your experience, you will probably apply a bandage which comes loose during work. It is hoped that this occurs when riding or schooling at home, and not at some outing of importance. Be aware of the potential danger of tripping caused by a loose bandage.

- Overtight bandages can cause a restriction in the blood supply to the leg. The risk is enhanced if the bandages get wet (e.g. going through water on a cross-country ride) and then dry out again, tightening onto the leg at the same time.

- Practise securing your bandages well, making sure that the tapes or Velcro are never tighter than the bandage itself.

- In general, exercise bandages should cover the region immediately below the knee to just around the fetlock joint (over the ergot but not under the joint).

- Padding under a bandage should be trimmed to just a few millimetres wider than the bandage itself.

Saddlery

The candidate should:

Know the correct principles and fitting of saddlery and bits in general use, including those used for training and competition work.

Know how to organise a saddle room and its contents.

Know how to clean and store saddlery and rugs.

ELEMENT

C **2.1.1** Demonstrate correct application and fitting of tack commonly used in dressage competitions.

C **2.1.2** Demonstrate correct application and fitting of tack commonly used in cross-country competitions.

S **2.2.1** Explain indications of incorrect fitting and/or inappropriate saddlery, and the possible consequences.

C **2.3.1** Explain the action of a variety of bits in general use.

C **2.4.1** Apply and fit a variety of boots used for protection, suitable for various competitions.

S **2.5.1** Describe the perfect tack room.

S **2.6.1** Give examples of appropriate practice for storing tack and rugs.

What the examiner is looking for

- You will be expected to fit tack appropriate for dressage and cross-country competitions. (Elements 2.1.1 and 2.1.2)

- For dressage you will be required to put on and fit a double bridle and a dressage saddle. (Element 2.1.1)

- For cross-country you will be expected to choose a bridle with a bit which might typically be used for cross-country (e.g. a Dutch gag/three-ringed bit, or a Pelham with rubber or laced reins). You may choose a breastplate and/or a martingale, and you will be expected to fit a cross-country surcingle. (Element 2.1.2)

- You will be asked questions about the fitting of the equipment you have put on. You must be prepared to discuss the implications of ill-fitting or inappropriate equipment. (For example, fitting a heavy quilted saddle pad under a saddle for cross-country would be inappropriate as it is too bulky and hot and has no means of attaching itself to the saddle; ill-fitting tack could cause discomfort or injury.) (Element 2.2.1)

- You may have to look at a variety of bits, and these should be familiar to you. Make sure you know which bits are permissible and which are banned in pure dressage competitions. (For example, a double bridle is not permitted until Elementary level and then optional until Advanced, when it becomes mandatory.) Be able to discuss the types of bit which might be used for cross-country riding and for first training a young horse. (Element 2.3.1)

- The examiner is likely to ask you to choose boots appropriate for a specific discipline or for work. (Element 2.4.1) You are often asked to fit one front boot and one hind boot. Always choose equipment that is familiar to you and that you have had some experience of using before.

- You may be asked to describe your ideal tack room. (Element 2.5.1)

- You may be asked to discuss how to store equipment, including rugs, which may not be in use for a period of time (e.g. storing turn-out rugs during the summer months). (Element 2.6.1)

How to become competent

- This is a challenging area of practical competence. You will only achieve competence by frequent repetition, to convey consistency through familiarity in carrying out the tasks.

- If you are not able to fit dressage and jumping saddles in your work placement or training situation, then you must go to a yard where these types of saddle are used regularly.

- Even if you are not regularly able to fit these more specialist saddles, take the time to find some source where you can see them applied and used.

BITS COMMONLY SEEN IN EVERYDAY USE

Rubber straight-bar snaffle

*Straight-bar snaffle, 'Happy Mouth' or Nathe
(synthetic material)*

Cheek snaffle

*Australian loose-ring cheek snaffle, often known
as a 'Fulmer'*

Half-cheek snaffle

German eggbutt snaffle (thick mouthpiece)

Eggbutt snaffle (thin mouthpiece)

French-link bit

*Wire-ring (loose ring) German snaffle
(thick mouthpiece)*

D snaffle, often known as a 'racing bit'

*German KK bit. Central 'lozenge'
in same plane as bit, so very mild.
Similar in action to a French-link*

Hanging cheek snaffle

- The basic rules for correct fitting of a saddle apply here, so consider the following checklist:

  • overall appearance – e.g. does the saddle look over-large/too small for the size and type of horse?

  • four fingers' width over the wither – confirmed by the fit once the rider is sitting on the saddle;

  • no restriction through tight contact over the shoulder;

  • daylight should be visible along the spine of the horse under the gullet of the saddle;

  • contact with the back, with as much of the bearing surface of the lining as possible.

These rules apply equally to dressage and jumping saddles.

- Always fit a saddle without a numnah or saddle cloth to allow you to see exactly where the saddle makes contact with the horse.

- Get used to managing your equipment efficiently as this indicates competence. Gather all the tack you need and place it close to the stable for easy working. If you have to waste time going back and forth to pick up things you have forgotten (e.g. the girth) you will not convey competence or that you are organised.

- Never leave a valuable saddle in an unsafe place (e.g. on a stable door where a horse could easily knock it off).

THREE SLIGHTLY 'STRONGER' BUT COMMONLY USED BITS

Mullen-mouth pelham with curb chain

Dr Bristol snaffle. The flat central plate, being angled, makes the bit more severe

Three-ring gag snaffle, also known as 'Dutch gag' or 'bubble bit'

- Make sure that you take every opportunity to look at what horses are wearing before and during competitions; notice:

  - how well the tack stands up to the job asked of it;

  - how well it has been fitted.

  - if poorly fitted, are there any signs of problems (e.g. boots rubbing)?

- Look at the types of numnah or saddle cloth that riders choose for cross-country riding and for dressage classes. If possible, speak to the riders and ask them to explain their choice of equipment.

- Notice the types of rein, bits and boots used for each discipline.

- Look in tack shops and saddlery catalogues to see what is currently on the market for various types of competitive work.

- Ask your instructor to show you how to apply and fit a double bridle and then practise as often as you can. Watch horses working in double bridles in competition. Observe the action of the bits and make sure you are clear on why double bridles are used. What additional features can they offer in the control of the horse that is more highly trained in dressage, or is stronger across country, or is being shown in formal classes (e.g. hunter classes)?

- You must be well practised in fitting a double bridle and know exactly how it is put together and when it is used (e.g. it is correct dress in some show classes, and may be compulsory/prohibited in certain dressage tests, as previously mentioned).

- Be familiar with fitting any type of saddle, though usually a dressage saddle and some kind of jumping saddle is what would be asked.

- Be familiar with every type of bit in everyday use. Ask questions and listen to sound opinions on the action and use of some bits in everyday life. The requirement of the bit must be for: control/safety/balance and coordination between horse and rider.

- Consider how you would construct your ideal tack room: what would you want in it for the organised, efficient and professional image that you wish to portray? Consider the size appropriate to the equipment to be stored. Think about security, flooring, storage facilities and sources of light, heat and water.

- Be able to discuss the storing of rugs and other equipment which might not be in current use. Consider how this is done in your yard.

- Ask colleagues and friends about the policy they adopt for the storing of rugs and out-of-season equipment.

- Be observant constantly, particularly at competitions, and notice the wide variety of equipment that is in use today.

- Make sure that you have been shown how to fit a cross-country surcingle or overgirth, and that you are quite sure you would recognise the equipment and know how to apply it.

Travelling Horses

Know the procedures when travelling horses by trailer or horsebox and safe procedures for loading and unloading.

ELEMENT

| C | **3.1.1** Carry out appropriate checks on transport vehicles to ensure the horses' safety and well-being during loading and transportation, and report any discrepancies. |

| C | **3.2.1** Carry out checks on the loading horses' clothing and report on its suitability. |

| S | **3.3.1** List equipment to be taken (water etc.). |

| S | **3.4.1** Explain to an assistant the loading procedure with regard to the safety of yourself, the horse and others. |

| S | **3.4.2** Explain to an assistant the unloading procedure with regard to the safety of yourself, the horse and others. |

| S | **3.5.1** Give examples of procedures for loading difficult horses with regard to the safety of yourself, the horse and others. |

| C | **3.6.1** Demonstrate how to safely load and secure a horse. |

| C | **3.6.2** Demonstrate how to safely unload a horse. |

What the examiner is looking for

- You will be asked to look at a vehicle (either a trailer attached to a towing vehicle or a horsebox). Often, as a group exercise, you will be expected to check the vehicle for its suitability for transporting one or more horses. (Element 3.1.1) The checks would fall into two broad categories:

    (a) the area where the horse(s) will stand – consider floor, roof, ventilation, amount of room per horse, standing configuration, ease of movement of partitions, tie rings.

(b) the roadworthiness of the vehicle – the road tax must be current, and the vehicle be insured for the driver; mention that the tyres should be checked, as should the lights and indicators; is there sufficient fuel for the journey? if a trailer has not been in recent or regular use the towing hitch should be checked.

- The horse to be loaded will already be 'dressed' to travel. Be able to discuss the suitability of the clothing. Consider the fit, the choice according to the weather, the length of the journey and how the horse travels. (Element 3.2.1) Be prepared to ask questions of the examiner to ascertain what answers you would give. (For example, 'Is the horse to be travelled on a summer's day?' If 'yes', a thin anti-sweat sheet to keep flies and dust off and offer slight protection against draughts is fine.)

- You may be asked to discuss the type of equipment you would need to take for travelling a horse to a competition. (Element 3.3.1)

- It is likely that you will be asked to brief one of the other candidates in your group on the procedure for loading and unloading a horse safely, showing clear awareness for the safety of yourself, the horse and anyone else in proximity. (Elements 3.4.1 and 3.4.2)

- You may be asked to discuss how you would assist the loading of a difficult horse. (Element 3.5.1)

- As a group you will be expected to competently load, secure and then unload a horse with awareness for everyone's safety. (Elements 3.6.1 and 3.6.2) Your loading and unloading procedure should demonstrate confidence and control of the horse at all times. You should be able to clearly direct the horse straight up the ramp and secure him with minimal fuss, closing the partition or ramp as relevant to ensure the horse's safety. (The horse you will be asked to load will always be straightforward and will load and unload quietly and with obedience.)

How to become competent

- Make sure that you have some knowledge of how to check a vehicle for suitability for travelling horses. The road requirements should be automatic, if you are already a car driver. The horse requirements relate to the safety of the vehicle for horses and their comfort when travelling.

- Look at any horseboxes or trailers that you have the opportunity to see. Whether they be pristine transporters at a local agricultural or county show, or a car and trailer that pulls into the yard in your training centre, take the trouble to look around them and see what features you think are horse friendly or not.

- You should already be familiar in your training or work situation with horses going to competitions. You should be used to equipping them for travelling (Stage 2), and now you will have to look at a horse already dressed and be sure that you are happy that the equipment is appropriate and fitted safely for the journey. Look at as many different situations as you can where horses are travelling; observe what they wear and ask questions where you can as to why a certain rug or leg protection has been chosen.

- Look in tack shops and catalogues at the wide range of equipment available for every type of situation of travelling horses.

- Consider what equipment and supplies would be necessary for even a short journey (e.g. water and haynet). Then consider the extra needs for a longer period away from home (e.g. feeds and extra rugs for an overnight stay). Talk to others who have experience of travelling horses.

- Be able to explain clearly to anyone who may be willing to help you load or unload a horse, what role you wish them to play in the procedure. It is important that whenever you are carrying out loading or unloading everyone involved knows where they are meant to be and what they are doing before starting the process.

- Safety and awareness is of paramount importance, both for horses and handlers. It is always safer, especially with a horse who may be unruly, to wear a hat and gloves for loading.

- Watch as many horses being loaded as you can. Try to observe the procedure in different circumstances (e.g. trailers and lorries). Take note of the methods that may be adopted if a horse is reluctant to load. Consider what measures can be taken to encourage a difficult horse to load or unload.

- Be aware of the possible need to control the horse with greater authority (bridle

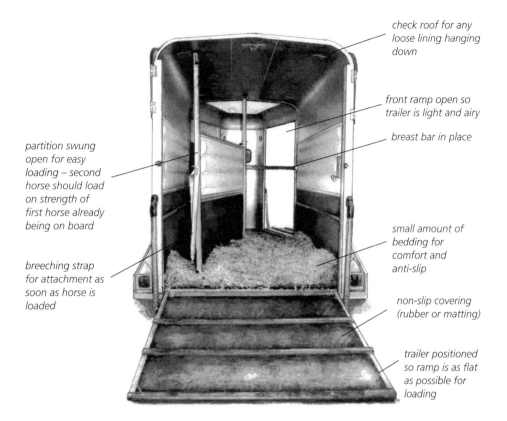

check roof for any
loose lining hanging
down

front ramp open so
trailer is light and airy

breast bar in place

partition swung
open for easy
loading – second
horse should load
on strength of
first horse already
being on board

small amount of
bedding for
comfort and
anti-slip

breeching strap
for attachment as
soon as horse is
loaded

non-slip covering
(rubber or matting)

trailer positioned
so ramp is as flat
as possible for
loading

Points to check on a trailer before travelling.

instead of headcollar or a chiffney to prevent the horse putting his head high to avoid the control from you).

- Assisting loading and unloading horses as often as you can so that you have confidence in maintaining authority over any horse that you are in charge of.

- Consider the best way to secure horses in trailers or lorries. Usually a rope to a piece of string attached to a tie ring in the vehicle is appropriate. The headcollar should be leather, and the rope easy to handle for tying.

- There is no substitute for practice when it comes to loading; it is something that you must do repeatedly, and preferably be as comfortable about loading/unloading a horse into and from a trailer as you do about loading and unloading into and from a lorry/horsebox.

- There are various little 'tricks of the trade' that could be utilised to encourage a horse that is difficult or reluctant to load. For example, as already mentioned, a bridle or chiffney will increase authority and control. A horse that is reluctant to walk up the ramp can be coaxed with a rope behind him, held on either side by two people – this shows him that the easiest way is to go forward up the ramp. A well-timed push on the backside with a yard broom can encourage a horse who is reluctant to move up the ramp; even a sprinkle of water on the horse's backside can encourage him to load. Always remember, though, that whatever method you choose, there is an element of risk that the horse may kick out in irritation or resistance and you and your assistant(s) must not be within range.

Lungeing

Lunge an experienced fit horse efficiently in an enclosed space.

ELEMENT

C	**4.1.1**	Use lunge equipment safely and to good effect.
C	**4.2.1**	Show a safe, appropriate lunge technique for an unknown horse.
C	**4.3.1**	Use exercises suitable for developing and maintaining control whilst exercising the horse.
C	**4.3.2**	Demonstrate an appropriate method of exercise, showing appreciation for the horse's balance and fitness level.
S	**4.4.1**	Demonstrate an understanding of the importance of rhythm and balance.
S	**4.5.1**	Explain the value of lungeing.
S	**4.6.1**	Describe the tack and facilities required.

What the examiner is looking for

- You were required to fit lunge equipment at Stage 2, so this knowledge should be secure. Now you should be able to glance at a horse equipped to lunge and be able to make any swift adjustment to ill-fitting or poorly applied tack. (Element 4.1.1)

- You will be expected to handle the lunge horse and the equipment provided competently and with familiarity. This enables you to demonstrate your ability to control an experienced fit horse, lungeing to exercise it to good effect. Your handling of the equipment must show safe, secure lungeing technique. (Element 4.2.1)

- The exercises you choose should work the horse sufficiently, as if the session you are doing is the horse's only exercise for that day. (Element 4.3.1)

- You must show work that establishes the horse's rhythm and balance, with the horse going forward but without being hurried. (Element 4.4.1)

- You are likely to be asked about the value of lungeing – its worth to the horse, when you might use it, how long you might lunge for, and where you would choose to lunge the horse. Appropriate lungeing equipment is also likely to be discussed and may relate to the horse you have actually worked. (Elements 4.5.1 and 4.6.1)

How to become competent

- There are no short-cuts to lungeing competence. Lungeing is an art like riding, and only practice and more practice will make you proficient.

- Even if you cannot lunge a horse very often, watch other people lungeing whenever you can.

- Practise the techniques for managing the lunge line and the whip (this does not have to be done with a horse). You can easily attach the end of the lunge line to a fence or ring; or ask a friend to hold the end of the rein while you practise paying the rein out, controlling the position of the whip, and gathering up the rein again, maintaining as level a contact on the rein as you can.

- When lungeing it is essential that you learn to put the horse out onto a contact on a circle of at least 15m, and preferably from 18m to 20m.

- The bigger the circle, the easier it is for the horse. Circles that are too small tend to encourage stiffness, and loss of rhythm and forwardness.

- Watch how more experienced people lunge and learn from them.

- The horse may be wearing a saddle or a roller, with a bridle and a lunge cavesson. It would be usual to have side-reins on the saddle in readiness for when the horse is going forward sufficiently. You should know that when lungeing a horse with a rider on top, the side-reins are purely to help keep the horse as straight as possible.

- The purpose of side-reins when exercising the horse is not only to keep the horse straight but also to give the horse a contact to work forward into. The side-reins

Horse 'dressed' for exercise on the lunge (without a rider).

should not be attached **until** the horse is going forward sufficiently. They are likely to inhibit forward movement if put on too soon and before the horse is truly forward.

- Be familiar with adjusting the side-reins to make them shorter or longer, but do not make this a long-drawn-out process when the horse may get increasingly fractious. It should not be necessary to undo the side-reins every time you change the rein or when you adjust them. As long as you are **aware** of the horse and can 'read' his possible anxiety or tension, then it is safe to adjust the side-reins. If the horse is showing tension and an indication that he will not stand quietly while you adjust the side-reins, then it would be wise to undo them while adjusting. At Stage 3 level you should be able to show this awareness and judgement.

- Your aim is to maintain a harmonious communication between you and the horse through your good handling of the equipment and your body language, which assists your voice in the control of the horse.

- Learn to use your voice in a positive and authoritative manner, in conjunction with your body language, to maintain control over the horse.

- Learn to maintain the horse's rhythm by developing a 'feel' for when to push the horse forward and when to 'hold hard' a little so as not to hassle the horse out of his natural rhythm.

- Be able to decrease and increase the size of the circle to work the horse further and encourage lateral suppleness. This, in conjunction with transitions from one pace to another, leads to activity, suppleness and obedience from the horse.

- Be able to make frequent transitions from one pace to another, as well as transitions within the pace, to encourage activity of the hind legs and obedience from the horse.

- Be able to talk about how long you might lunge a fit horse – 20 to 30 minutes, including the three basic gaits. The length of work on the lunge would be relevant to the horse's age, fitness, the ground conditions on which he was working, and the weather.

- Be able to talk with confidence about the lungeing cavesson, stating what you like and dislike about it (e.g. easy to lunge off both reins with minimal effort because the rein acts from a central ring; cumbersome and best fitted without the bridle noseband, but firm so that the heavy noseband does not rub or slip).

- Describe the lunge rein. (For instance, it could be webbing; or it could be a rope with a clip attachment at the end.)

- Be able to discuss the value of lungeing. There are quite a number of reasons, such as:
    - You can work the horse harder in a shorter period of time – useful if you are very busy and have little time to school.
    - You can work a horse that you might otherwise be too tall or too heavy to school on his back.
    - If a horse is not yet broken to saddle, lungeing would be the way to start work.

- The ideal place to lunge a horse is in an outdoor or indoor school that is completely enclosed and with an artificial surface. If this is not possible or practical you need to find a quiet corner of a field that has few distractions around, and cordon off an area with a few poles and blocks to make a small corral. This would present an illusion of being enclosed, which should give you a modicum more control if the horse is sharp or somewhat full of himself.

- In most cases, to lunge a horse to good effect it is usually necessary to work it in walk, trot and canter evenly on both reins. At this level you must feel confident to canter a horse on the lunge if you feel it would help him.

- In lungeing, as in riding, an important piece of advice is that you **must** have regular practice to develop the necessary feel and awareness.

Stable Design

The candidate should be able to:

Understand simple planning of the stable yard and the advantages and disadvantages of different types of stabling and fittings.

ELEMENT

C   **5.1.1** Describe the perfect stable yard.

C   **5.2.1** Give examples of good ventilation systems.

C   **5.2.2** Give examples of good drainage systems.

S   **5.3.1** Outline the advantages and disadvantages of keeping horses in a traditional stable yard.

S   **5.3.2** Outline the advantages and disadvantages of keeping horses in an American barn-style stable yard.

S   **5.4.1** Give the advantages and disadvantages of prefabricated wooden stables.

C   **5.5.1** Identify areas of importance when allocating stabling to specific horses.

S   **5.6.1** Give examples of labour-saving stable fittings/devices.

What the examiner is looking for

- You will usually be asked to look at the stable yard where you are taking your exam, and this will be covered in the practical oral section of the exam. (Element 5.1.1)

- Be able to discuss the stables you see against an ideal. (Element 5.1.1)

- When thinking of the perfect stable yard, consider the following: size of stables; their configuration (e.g. straight line, quadrangle, or barn style); the materials from which the stables might be made; lighting; ventilation; access; flooring;

drainage; and fittings. You may be asked to discuss one or more of these topics. (Element 5.1.1)

- For horses, a good size of stable is in the region of 12ft by 14ft (3.6m x 4.6m), bigger is needed for broodmares, and smaller is acceptable for ponies.

- Be able to recognise natural ventilation, and also doors and windows which have been designed to allow good air circulation. (Element 5.2.1) Consider the position of windows in relation to doors – it is the flow of air that is important when considering ventilation. A draught over the horse's back is as likely to cause possible health problems as a stuffy stable with poor air circulation.

- You may be asked to look at the stable floor and decide what type of drainage is present. (Element 5.2.2) Be able to discuss other methods of drainage that you may have seen.

- Consider whether the stable floor slopes, if it does at all. If it slopes to the back, front or centre then look there to see if there is a corresponding drain.

- Old-fashioned stables often had 'stable brick' floors. These were anti-slip, 'warm' and aided drainage. On the down side, they would now be prohibitively expensive to lay down and labour-intensive to manage (difficult to sweep).

- When asked about the 'traditional stable yard' you should consider how the stables may be sited (in a straight line, or forming a two-, three- or four-sided yard).

- Notice whether there is a concrete 'apron' in front of the stables, an overhang from the roof, and any means of enclosing the stables safely. Be able to discuss the advantages and disadvantages as you see them. (Element 5.3.1)

- When considering the advantages and disadvantages of American barn-style stables, make sure that you have some ideas for and against. (Element 5.3.2)

- You may be asked about wooden stables, particularly if these are present in the yard in which you are working. (Element 5.4.1)

- Wooden stables are reasonably cheap and easy to erect, but they are not hard-wearing, especially if your horses like chewing wood; and they can be stuffy in summer if the ventilation is not good.

- Consider access: doors must be wide (4ft/1.2m at least) and high enough

(7ft/2.3m), although it is remarkable how horses can adapt, so comment on this but do not be over-condemning if a horse is living in a stable with a very low access. The chances are he is happy and quite used to it.

- You will be asked to discuss how to choose specific stables for specific horses. (Element 5.5.1) Make sure that you can talk about broodmares needing bigger stables, nervous or young horses needing near contact with other horses so that they do not feel isolated, and horses that may thrive more in outside stables rather than in an American barn.

- You are likely to be asked about labour-saving stable fittings. (Element 5.6.1) Basic fittings such as tie rings (for tying horses or haynets) are essential for efficient yard management, while the availability of automatic water and fitted mangers is also essential to some people.

How to become competent

- You will be familiar with the yard in which you work. Have you tried looking

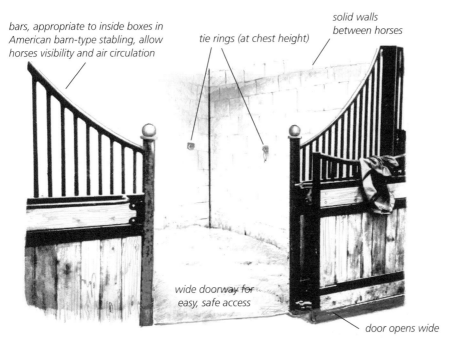

bars, appropriate to inside boxes in American barn-type stabling, allow horses visibility and air circulation

tie rings (at chest height)

solid walls between horses

wide doorway for easy, safe access

door opens wide

A 12ft x 14ft (3.6m x 4.6m) internal stable – a good size. This stable has rubber flooring overlaid with a small amount of bedding for comfort and cleanliness.

around your yard in an objective way, to see how many advantages and disadvantages you can find?

- You should take every opportunity to look at as many different stable yards as you can. Ask yard workers what they like and don't like about their set-up.

- You can learn from every yard you see; and even visits to trade stands at horse and agricultural shows where stables might be on show can be helpful.

- Most equestrian colleges have an American barn-style stable unit, because for large numbers of horses they are the most economic and labour-saving. If you have no experience of such a unit, make an effort to go and look at one and see how it works.

- In any stable you have access to, look at the floor and see whether there is any visible sign of drainage. There may be a slope on the floor towards a front or rear drain, there may be a central drain with herringbone ridging or a gentle slope taking the wet towards the middle.

- Consider doors, width and access from outside, look at windows, do they open or only provide light, are they protected if they are glass?

- Consider fittings, water systems are all slightly different, how many rings are there? Is there a fixed manger or a manger holder and does this have access from the outside of the stable (i.e. without opening the door – this would be very labour-saving in a big yard)?

- Always consider the yard as a whole. Where is the muck heap? Is the approach up-hill or level? (It's hard work to push wheelbarrows uphill!) What is the yard made of? (Gravel looks smart but is hard to sweep!)

- Talk to people who work in different yards and find out what their likes and dislikes are in the yard in which they work. Looks can be deceptive. A yard which looks super might, in reality, be difficult to manage when you work there day-by-day (e.g. hanging baskets around the yard look lovely in summer, but horses can eat them easily if they are in reach and they take a great deal of watering to keep them looking good).

- Gain as much experience as you can in looking at different stable units and be able to talk about what you see.

Anatomy and Physiology

Know basic good and bad conformation.

Know the horse's main trunk muscles used to support his limbs and to support and carry his rider.

Know the basic structure of the leg below the knee/hock.

Know the basic outline of the horse's respiratory and circulatory systems.

Recognise basic causes of lameness and know their treatments.

ELEMENT

S	**6.1.1**	Discuss a presented horse's general proportions with regard to conformation.
S	**6.1.2**	Discuss normal and abnormal forelimb conformation.
S	**6.1.3**	Discuss normal and abnormal hind limb conformation.
S	**6.1.4**	Discuss how the presented horse's conformation may affect his way of going.
S	**6.2.1**	Show and name the horse's main superficial muscles.
C	**6.3.1**	Name the tendons in a forelimb.
S	**6.3.2**	Show where the individual tendons run.
C	**6.4.1**	Name the ligaments found in a forelimb.
S	**6.4.2**	Show where the individual ligaments are.
S	**6.5.1**	Identify the sesamoid bones and describe their function.
S	**6.6.1**	Designate the respiratory tract and/or the basic function of each section.

C	**6.6.2** Identify a horse's respiration rate.
C	**6.6.3** Describe the symptoms of respiratory problems in the horse.
S	**6.7.1** Give a basic description of the function of the main parts of the circulatory system.
C	**6.7.2** Explain the functions of the circulatory system.
S	**6.7.3** Explain how the heart rate can be a fitness indicator.
C	**6.7.4** Give examples of dealing with circulatory problems such as arterial bleeding from a wound, and filled legs.
C	**6.8.1** Identify and/or designate bony enlargements such as splints.
C	**6.8.2** Identify and/or designate bursal enlargements on the horse's limbs.
C	**6.8.3** Name and give the causes, symptoms and treatments of bursal enlargements, tendon and ligament strains and bony enlargements found in the horse's lower limb.

What the examiner is looking for

- This section will be examined in a stable yard, in a group, with up to five candidates at a time working with one examiner.

- A horse will be stood up in the stable, or outside if the weather is good, and the group will be expected to talk about the horse's conformation. (Element 6.1.1)

- Conformation relates to the bone structure of the horse. You should first look at the overall picture of the horse and then try to assess the individual parts.

- You should be able to recognise basic good and bad points of conformation, particularly in relation to the fore and hind limbs. (Elements 6.1.2 and 6.1.3)

- You may be asked to talk about how you think faults in the horse's conformation might affect his way of going (e.g. if the horse has a very upright shoulder he may have a short, choppy stride). (Element 6.1.4)

- You will be asked to name and indicate on a horse the location of the superficial muscles of the horse's body and the main tendons and ligaments in the legs. (Elements 6.2.1, 6.3.1, 6.3.2, 6.4.1 and 6.4.2) You may also be required to

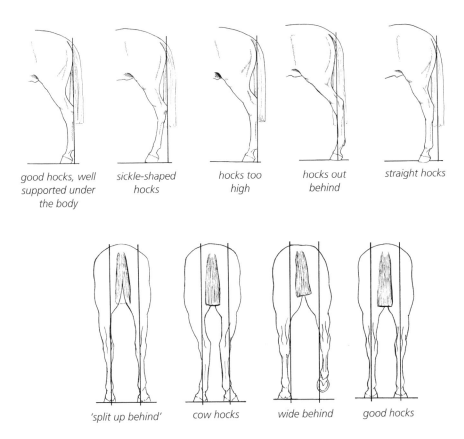

good hocks, well supported under the body · sickle-shaped hocks · hocks too high · hocks out behind · straight hocks

'split up behind' · cow hocks · wide behind · good hocks

identify and describe the function of the sesamoid bones. (Element 6.5.1)

■ As a group you will be asked to show where the horse's respiratory tract is, which are the main parts and how these function. (Element 6.6.1)

■ When asked about the respiratory tract and also about the circulatory system, its parts and function, it is important that you can pick up the discussion at any point, so that you can carry on from where another candidate has stopped. (Elements 6.7.1 and 6.7.2)

■ You will be asked the horse's respiratory rate, which at rest is in the range of 8 to 12 breaths per minute. You must learn this and remember it. (Element 6.6.2)

■ You may also be asked how the heart rate can be a fitness indicator. An unfit horse has to breathe faster to supply enough oxygen to his muscles to metabolise into energy. As he becomes fitter his cardio-vascular system becomes more efficient

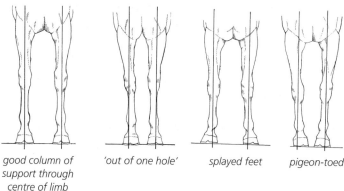

good column of   'out of one hole'   splayed feet   pigeon-toed
support through
centre of limb

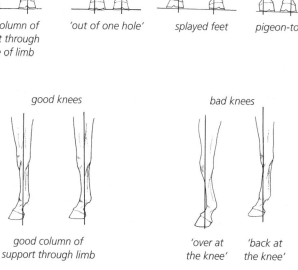

good knees   bad knees

good column of   'over at   'back at
support through limb   the knee'   the knee'

and therefore does not have to work so hard, the heart rate is therefore lower when the horse works and the recovery after work is quicker. (Element 6.7.3)

- You may be asked to describe some conditions that arise as a result of circulatory problems. (Element 6.7.4) You must be able to talk about filled legs and how you would deal with this condition, and how you might treat acute bleeding, perhaps from an artery, until the vet arrives.

- You will be asked to show on the horse's legs where splints occur. (Element 6.8.1) You may be asked about other bony enlargements and you should know where they occur. (Make sure that bone spavin, sesamoiditis, ringbone and sidebone are all familiar to you.)

- You may be asked to show on the limbs where bursal enlargements or soft tissue swellings are found. (Element 6.8.2) (Make sure you know where bog spavin, thoroughpins, windgalls and curbs appear.)

- You may be asked to talk about symptoms and treatments of any soft tissue swelling, bursal or bony enlargements and tendon or ligament strains.

- The horse that is presented for this section of the exam is usually one that has plenty of wear and tear on his limbs and exhibits some of the more easily recognised 'lumps and bumps'.

- The horse used for conformation is often one that is not blessed with good bone structure, so it should be easy for you to find some faults.

How to become competent

- When trying to develop an 'eye' for strengths and weaknesses in conformation, you cannot look at too many horses.

- Learn to look at the horse from a slight distance to get an 'overview' of the horse. Try to recognise the basic proportions of the horse. Does his head match his body for size, does his back look very long or his neck rather short in proportion to the rest of his body? Look more closely at each part of the horse and learn to recognise good and poor areas of conformation.

- Understand terms such as 'upright shoulder', 'over at the knee', and 'cow hocks'.

- Try to look at horses in the presence of someone who is experienced in assessing conformation – this may be your instructor or someone who judges showing classes and has great ability to consider strengths and weaknesses in the horse's build.

- Consider the horse's limbs. Look at the forelimbs from the front and assess the 'column of support', i.e. the way the limb is aligned, by dropping an imaginary vertical (plumb) line from the centre of the shoulder down the front of each forelimb to the ground.

- Look at the hind legs in the same way. Be able to discuss deviations of any of the limbs from the true vertical line and consider how these deviations might put strain on other parts of the limb.

- Consider how weaknesses in conformation might affect the horse's way of going. Speak to your vet and find out what sort of leg injuries he treats and what are the commonest causes of those injuries. Spending a day travelling around with a

*SUPERFICIAL MUSCLES
(FRONT VIEW)*

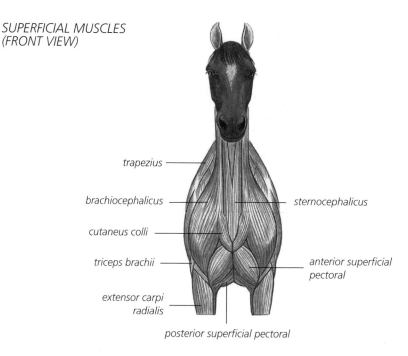

trapezius

brachiocephalicus

cutaneus colli

triceps brachii

extensor carpi
radialis

sternocephalicus

anterior superficial
pectoral

posterior superficial pectoral

horse vet can be another excellent way of learning about make and shape of horses, action, injuries and treatments.

■ It may be difficult to learn the names of the superficial muscles but these are something you must be familiar with and be able to pronounce:

- masseter, rhomboideus, splenius, trapezius, sternocephalicus, brachio-cephalicus – all in the head and neck

- deltoid, triceps, superficial pectoral, radial carpal extensor, common digital extensor, lateral carpal extensor – all in the shoulder and forearm

- latissimus dorsi, intercostal, longissimus dorsi, deep pectoral – in the back or barrel region of the horse

- gluteal fascia or superficial, semitendinosus, biceps femoris, deep digital flexor and digital extensor – all in the hindquarters

■ Understanding the way the muscles function is important. The principle that muscles work essentially in pairs and that muscles have points of origin or insertion onto a bone, sometimes through the attachment of a tendon, should also be understood.

SUPERFICIAL MUSCLES

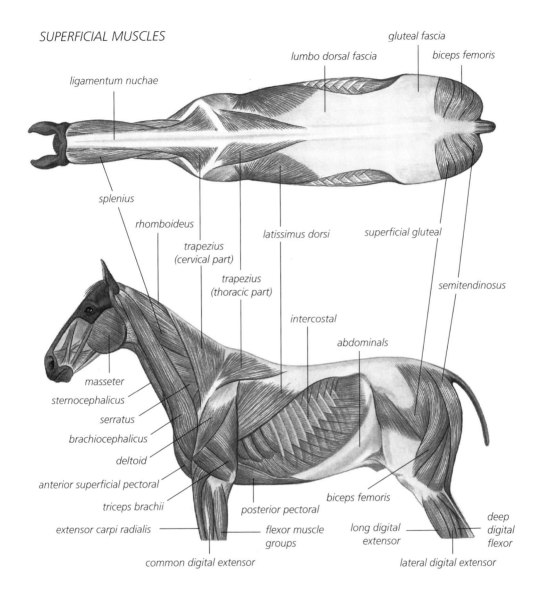

gluteal fascia

lumbo dorsal fascia

biceps femoris

ligamentum nuchae

splenius

rhomboideus

trapezius
(cervical part)

trapezius
(thoracic part)

latissimus dorsi

superficial gluteal

semitendinosus

intercostal

abdominals

masseter

sternocephalicus

serratus

brachiocephalicus

deltoid

anterior superficial pectoral

triceps brachii

posterior pectoral

biceps femoris

deep
digital
flexor

extensor carpi radialis

flexor muscle
groups

long digital
extensor

common digital extensor

lateral digital extensor

- As a competent Stage 3 candidate you should be able to describe the siting of the superficial muscles of the horse with a basic understanding of how they enable the horse to move.

- You must understand the difference between the basic action of a muscle, a tendon and a ligament.

- In the same way as you have learned to identify the muscles, you must learn the

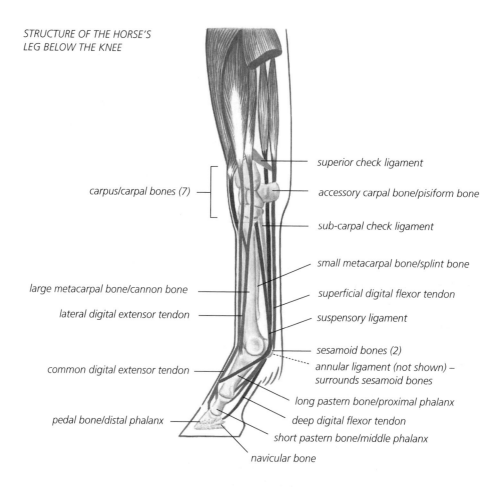

STRUCTURE OF THE HORSE'S LEG BELOW THE KNEE

carpus/carpal bones (7)

superior check ligament

accessory carpal bone/pisiform bone

sub-carpal check ligament

small metacarpal bone/splint bone

large metacarpal bone/cannon bone

superficial digital flexor tendon

lateral digital extensor tendon

suspensory ligament

sesamoid bones (2)

annular ligament (not shown) – surrounds sesamoid bones

common digital extensor tendon

long pastern bone/proximal phalanx

deep digital flexor tendon

pedal bone/distal phalanx

short pastern bone/middle phalanx

navicular bone

main tendons and ligaments in the lower limbs. Be able to name them confidently and also to indicate on the horse's leg where each tendon or ligament runs.

- Be sure that you know where the superior check ligament, the sub-carpal check ligament and the suspensory ligaments run.

- Be familiar with the position of the superficial digital flexor tendon, the deep digital flexor tendon, the lateral digital extensor tendon and the common digital extensor tendon.

- In studying the lower limb it is as well to remember the bones: cannon bone, two splint bones, two sesamoid bones, how the shape of the fetlock joint is formed, the long pastern bone, the short pastern bone, the coffin or pedal bone and the navicular bone.

- It is sometimes interesting to compare the anatomy of the human limb with that of the horse to see how the horse's limb has evolved into a 'one-toed' creature from the original five digits present in our own limbs.

- The points of origin and insertion of the ligaments and tendons should be known, with a basic understanding of how the limb is motivated by the tendons and ligaments in conjunction with the muscles in the upper limb.

- Remember the basic anatomy of the skeleton which you covered in Stage 2 and be aware of the sesamoid bones. They play a major part in the structure of the fetlock joint and have a close relationship with the main tendons and ligaments in the limb.

- Learn the relevant parts of the respiratory and circulatory systems. You will need to be able to explain (with the horse in front of you) how air is taken into the nostrils, and ultimately into the lungs, what happens in the lung tissue and how air is expelled. From this you must then understand the link between the air taken into the lungs and the use of the oxygen by the body – how oxygen is transported around the body and how waste carbon dioxide is then expelled.

- You should understand the basic difference between arteries and veins, and be able to discuss the structure and function of the heart.

- You can find information on the circulatory and respiratory systems in *The BHS Veterinary Manual*. Once you have learned the information, repeatedly practise describing the systems and the way they work.

- Remember: you may be asked to pick up a discussion half-way through, and this is another thing you must be confident about.

- Always be sure to listen to other candidates so that you can add to or disagree with their statement if you feel there is more to say or an incorrect answer has been given.

- The reason for learning about the horse's systems is to enhance your awareness that a possible problem is arising. By understanding when the horse is functioning 'correctly' it is much easier to recognise any small deviation from normal and take necessary action before a problem develops.

- Be able to discuss basic faults in both the circulatory and the respiratory systems. Faults such as 'filled legs' may be visible on one of the horses you have in the stable management part of the exam. Make sure you have studied why filled legs occur and what you should do to 'manage' them or prevent them developing.

- As your experience develops you are likely to have seen or already taken care of a horse whose legs fill. Thus you should know that gentle activity will usually reduce the thickening.

- Be able to recognise profuse bleeding and know that this may be from an artery. In such cases the vet must be called as soon as possible, as the bleeding may need professional help to stop it.

- Recognise that different methods of improving fitness suit different horses, but the main aim of fittening is to develop the horse's cardio-vascular system so that he can do more work more easily and recover more quickly, therefore exposing his body to less stress.

- Try to learn from others who fitten horses for specific disciplines, e.g. eventing or point-to-point racing. It is valuable to back up your theoretical knowledge with some practical information gained from riders who have actually worked towards or competed in any equestrian discipline.

- Be aware that the speed of recovery of the horse from a short, sharp canter will tell you a lot about his fitness and stamina.

- You will be asked to point out on the horse in front of you sites of injury, lumps, bumps and blemishes.

- Look at as many different horses as you can, preferably with a more experienced person beside you – they can point out things that you may miss.

- Be clear on the type of injury that is likely to occur after working a horse persistently on hard ground (e.g. bony problems brought about by excessive jarring – typically splints, sesamoiditis, pedalostitis, ring bone, or bone spavin). Similarly be aware that soft tissue injuries, strains and sprains are more likely to result from stress in heavy or deep going, or from sudden stress when galloping from hard to soft ground or vice versa (bog spavins, thoroughpins, muscle, tendon or ligament injuries, pulls and strains.) Windgalls can arise generally as a result of work stress. They can be associated with hard or soft ground but often arise during the summer when the ground gets a little hard.

COMMON SITES OF INJURY AND BLEMISH   * = soft swelling/bursal enlargement

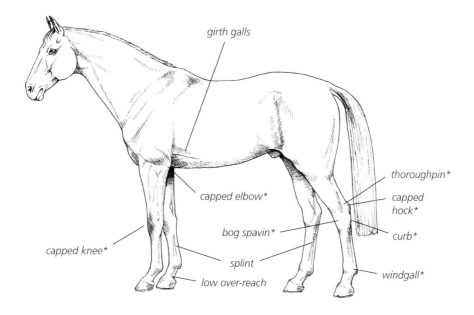

- Feel confident that you can discuss basic first aid for any of the problems that you may have already identified.

- Always be prepared to suggest that if, after a limited time of your own 'first aid', there is no improvement in the condition (e.g. after hosing a wound to cleanse it and begin to constrict the blood vessels, the blood is still flowing), then you would call the vet.

- Practise looking at legs for blemishes. Remember to let the horse know you are there, before feeling the blemish to see whether it is soft (usually bursal) or hard (usually bony).

- Always consider the horse's response to your touch: he may be showing discomfort if you apply pressure to a blemish, or he may be just reacting to the sensation (to the pressure but not to pain). To be sure, compare the response to pressure on one leg with an equal amount of pressure on the other leg.

- In most cases the treatment of any injury which causes the horse to be lame is a relative period of rest.

The Horse's Foot

Understand good foot conformation and the effects of poor hoof balance.

ELEMENT

C **7.1.1** Identify good/poor aspects of the balance of a horse's front feet.

S **7.2.1** Describe and show a horse's hoof-pastern axis.

S **7.2.2** Describe the possible problems caused by an incorrect hoof-pastern axis.

S **7.3.1** Identify indications of the horse's health and way of going by the state of wear of his shoes.

What the examiner is looking for

- The key word here is 'observation', and you must be able to describe what you see. There may be a group of up to five of you discussing one horse, and you must be prepared to say what you think and not be affected by what anyone else says: they may be wrong while you are right.

- To be able to identify good or poor foot balance you must be clear on the principles of foot balance and be able to apply them in practice to the horse that you are looking at. (Element 7.1.1)

- First, look at the horse's feet from in front. Do you see a pair of feet (both feet more or less matching)? Do not be distracted if one foot is white horn and one black or mixed colours – this can sometimes detract from your ability to compare the shape and size of the feet.

- Then cast your eye up the limb to the shoulder and back down, and try to draw an imaginary line down the centre of the limb, from the middle of the front of the shoulder to the ground. Ideally this line should equally divide the limb and the foot.

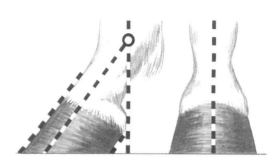

Balanced foot and good hoof-pastern axis from side and front view.

Lines demonstrating good balance and alignment of shoulder to pastern angle.

- Look at a similar vertical line from the side down the limb. From these two lines you can see how the horse's weight is distributed over his foot (from side to side and front to back).

You can then talk about the balance of the foot because you have been able to assess where he puts his weight over his foot (feet).

- Be able to show where the hoof-pastern axis is and know whether its angle to the ground is likely to induce possible problems in the horse's action. (Elements 7.2.1/7.2.2)

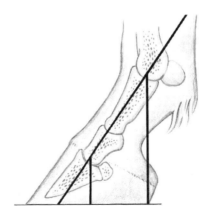

Bones of the lower limb. Lines marked demonstrate good alignment and foot balance.

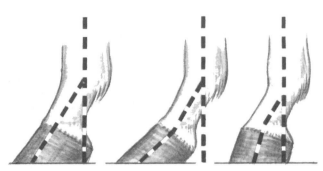

good hoof-pastern axis

broken back hoof-pastern axis; puts strain on the back of the leg

broken forward hoof-pastern axis subjects lower limb and foot to more concussion

- The hoof-pastern axis should be continuous. If it is broken forward or broken back this may cause problems through uneven weight distribution in the leg.

- You may be asked to comment on the condition of the horse's shoes. Be able to tell approximately how long ago the horse was shod and whether there are indications to its way of going by the wear on the shoes (e.g. worn toes on the hind shoes may mean that the horse is lazy behind and drags his toes). (Element 7.3.1)

- Be able to comment on brittle horn, old nail holes that are visible and have not closed up, cracks in the foot (those from the coronet being much more sinister potentially than cracks from the ground up), and ridges in the horn growth (showing possible changes in the horse's diet, if the horn colour changes, or possible laminitic changes if the horn is actually ridged).

How to become competent

- Watch farriers at work as often as you can. Ideally talk to the farriers who regularly visit your yard; ask many questions to enhance your knowledge of this field.

- The hoof-pastern axis, which runs from the fetlock joint through the long and short pastern bones and into the foot, should be a continuous line, on an angle of about 45° in the front foot, and a little steeper (50°) behind.

- In studying conformation (as discussed in Elements 6.1.1, 6.1.2 and 6.1.3) you should be familiar with looking at the hoof-pastern axis in relation to the angle of the shoulder in the upper limb.

Looking at limb alignment from in front. A vertical line is taken from the front of the shoulder to the ground through the forelimb.

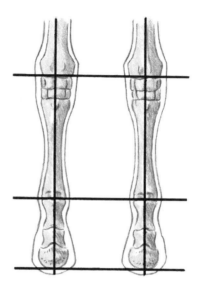

- In considering foot balance, your aim is to be able to assess whether the horse takes equal weight across his foot from side to side and similar equal weight from back to front. In this way the horse's body weight will come evenly down all four limbs and be distributed over the full weight-bearing surface of the foot.

- You should be able to tell whether the shoe enhances foot balance or impedes it in any way (e.g. tight heels on the shoe cause the shoe to 'constrict' the foot, which over a long period of time would have a detrimental effect).

- Be able to recognise an upright pastern and a sloping pastern and consider the possible weaknesses in action that these two extremes may cause. (Upright pasterns subject the foot to more concussion, while sloping ones put the tendons and ligaments at more risk of strains when the going is deep or inconsistent.)

- Try to feel in your riding, also, the difference in the 'ride' that a horse with upright feet will give you compared to one with a more sloping hoof-pastern axis.

- Look at as many different horses' feet and shoes as you can. Never miss an opportunity to look at feet, and pick them up, if possible.

- Get used to assessing the state of horses' shoes. Learn to recognise the signs of a recently shod foot compared to those of a foot that needs shoeing, and consider the amount of wear on the shoes.

- Remember that these days many horses do much of their work on an artificial surface, so their shoes will not show anything like the wear that they would if they were doing daily road work. You may have to rely more on the signs of growth in the foot and the beginnings of the clenches becoming loose, which would tell you that the shoe had been on for some weeks.

- Adopt a policy of looking at horses while they are standing still and trying to decide how they might move. Observe a horse at halt and then, if possible, watch him move. Your initial thoughts about the horse may be reinforced, or you may want to contradict them in the light of seeing how he actually moves.

- Remember that any opinions you may have about how good or poor conformation may affect the way the horse moves, and what this might predispose him to in the future, are pure speculation. It is always wise therefore to 'suggest' that the horse 'might' suffer certain problems. Always cover yourself and be diplomatic; don't make categorical statements, such as 'the horse has upright pasterns and therefore it will suffer from whatever'.

- In discussing hoof-pastern axis be able to discuss the 'broken forward' pastern and the 'broken back' pastern, knowing what each weakness in conformation may predispose the horse towards.

- Be able to assess limb alignment by looking at the front legs and drawing an imaginary line from the centre of the front of the shoulder down to the ground.

Shoeing

Know what to look for in a well-shod foot. Special shoes for special cases. Use of foot-pads and studs. Recognise faulty shoeing and know the consequent ill-effects.

ELEMENT

C **8.1.1** Describe the characteristics of a well-shod foot.

S **8.2.1** Explain the purpose of a variety of shoes including hunter shoes, rolled toes, feather-edged, wide web shoes.

C **8.3.1** Give examples of what you would not want to see in a newly shod foot and why.

S **8.4.1** Give examples of when to use pads.

C **8.5.1** Describe where to fit studs and how you keep stud holes in good order.

S **8.5.2** Give examples of appropriate studs for a variety of ground conditions.

What the examiner is looking for

- This section is examined in a group, with up to five of you discussing one horse.

- You may be asked to pick up a front or hind foot and describe what you see. (Element 8.1.1) The way in which you approach the horse is always taken into consideration, so make sure he knows you are there, particularly before you pick up a foot.

- Systematically describe the foot as you see it. Is the foot a pleasing shape appropriate to the size of the horse; is the horn, at first glance, in good condition?

- On picking up the foot what does the shoe look like? Is it newly shod? Are there signs that the shoe has been on for some time – with the foot beginning to overgrow the shoe, the clenches rising, and the heels beginning to look a little tight? Or is the shoe actually loose and perhaps quite worn?

- You may be asked to discuss what you would not wish to see against the 'ideal' for a newly shod foot. (Elements 8.1.1 and 8.3.1)

- The newly shod foot should present a picture of neatness, with the shoe fitting the foot, the clenches flush with the foot, and not too much sign of rasping.

- There may be a variety of shoes on a table or loose for you to pick out. Be able to identify some of the shoes that may be regarded as 'remedial' or 'specialist' shoes.

- You may be asked to identify shoes, such as rolled toes, wide web, feather-edged or traditional hunter type. (Element 8.2.1) Make sure that you are aware of which shoes have fallen out of use and what they were used for, and which your farrier would still apply and for what reason.

- You should be able to recognise if a shoe has stud holes in it, and you may be asked about how to maintain these. (Element 8.5.1)

- Understand what types of stud are used for different conditions. (Element 8.5.2)

- Tapping out stud holes regularly to maintain the thread on the hole so that the studs can be easily screwed in when needed, is something you will have either done yourself or have seen done, so you should feel able to talk about the procedure. The holes are usually kept plugged with cotton wool to keep them from filling with debris, which would make them difficult to use.

- Be able to recognise pads either in situ on the horse's feet or if handed to you. Understand why and when pads may be used. (Element 8.4.1)

- Pads are sometimes used as anti-concussion measures, or to protect the sole if it is rather flat and vulnerable to bruising. Pads can also be used to raise the heel to influence the balance of the foot and reduce pressure on the back of the foot and therefore on the back tendons in the leg.

How to become competent

- This section requires that you study the work of your farrier carefully and regularly.

- Make sure that you can competently recognise the characteristics of a well-shod foot (e.g. shoe fitting the foot snugly, well-positioned nails, with the clenches smooth and flush with the wall, plenty of weight-bearing surface of the shoe, heels long enough).

- Similarly, be able to discuss features of shoeing that you would prefer not to see (e.g. too much rasping of the wall, the toe cut back ('dumped'), the heels short and pinching).

- In being able to recognise or discuss faults in the well-shod foot, make sure that you can discuss why these faults would be detrimental to the horse.

- Ask your farrier about when he might use pads and how they are fitted between the shoe and the foot.

- Some pads cover the whole foot; some are inserted between the wall and the shoe and maybe cover the heel region.

- Some pads are anti-concussive, and some actually affect the balance of the foot (e.g. by raising the heels).

- Some farriers do not like studs, feeling that they affect the balance of the foot adversely; others fit them well forward, away from the heel.

- Make sure that you have looked at the different shapes of studs available for competition work. The chunky, squarer studs are for heavier more holding ground, and the more pointed studs are more suitable for hard ground.

- Make sure that you can identify small road studs, which may be permanently set in the shoes or can be screwed in, to prevent slipping on tarmac. Some people still have a preference for these if doing a lot of road work with their horses.

- If you have never seen any specialist shoes (many of which are not so common today) then study them in a book or try to find someone who can show you some different shoes.

- When looking at a shoe that you do not recognise, work out how it will fit the foot. Consider the shape of it (which should tell you whether it is a hind or a front shoe), consider where the nail holes are and how many there are (e.g. in a feather-edged shoe most of the nail holes will be on the outside of the shoe and the inner edge is tapered or 'feathered' with only a couple of nail holes to secure it, so allowing the shoe to be worn by a horse whose front or hind legs interfere.)

Action

The candidate should be able to:

Know the sequence of the horse's footfalls at all gaits; good and faulty action.

Identify foreleg/hind limb lameness.

ELEMENT

S	**9.1.1** Describe to an assistant the 'trotting up' procedure.
C	**9.1.2** Demonstrate how to 'trot a horse up'.
S	**9.2.1** Identify basic qualities and faults in movement using correct terminology.
C	**9.3.1** Describe the horse's posture and action when lame on a forelimb.
C	**9.3.2** Describe the horse's posture and action when lame on a hind limb.

What the examiner is looking for

- Handling the horse well is a priority in this part of the examination.

- You will be asked to 'trot the horse up' as if for inspection for a veterinary surgeon or a prospective purchaser. (Element 9.1.2)

- When instructing another person on how to trot the horse up, you must demonstrate your knowledge by the clarity of the instructions you give. (Element 9.1.1)

- The horse must be trotted up with competence, efficiency and rhythm. Imagine that a vet or potential buyer is looking at the horse – it is impossible to assess action if the horse is lazy, dragging its feet or losing rhythm.

- Find out where the horse is to be trotted up, and decide on whether to bring the horse out on a headcollar or a bridle (if in doubt use a bridle). Then give clear instructions to your assistant so that the horse is presented in walk up to and away from the viewer and similarly in trot.

- If the horse is lazy, be prepared to give some verbal assistance, or put yourself in a safe position where you can encourage the horse to go forward from behind.

- Make sure your assistant is told to turn the horse away from him/her, and to maintain a light contact on the rein(s) or lead rope, not one which in any way could interfere with the horse's natural balance and carriage.

- While the horse is being trotted up, the examiner will want to see you looking at the horse at all times. You can still speak to the examiner without making eye contact. Your eyes must be on the horse particularly during the turn, because here the horse may show an irregularity which is not visible on the flat.

- The examiner will expect you to be able to talk about the horse's action during the 'trot up'.

- You must know if the horse is sound or in any way not completely level in its walk and/or trot. (Elements 9.3.1 and 9.3.2)

- Make sure that you have learned terms such as 'plaiting' and 'toe in' and that you understand what they mean. You need to able to describe the way the horse moves towards you and away from you, if the examiner wants you to.

How to become competent

- Practise trotting up horses: some are easy; others can be sharp and full of themselves. In your exam you need to feel really confident about trotting the horse up yourself or instructing someone to do it for you.

- Look at the way the horse moves, from in front, from the side and from behind.

- Often the horse may have quite different action in the hind limbs as compared to the front limbs.

- Consider the regularity of the gait and also listen to the footfall. Feeling or hearing the footfall will help you recognise whether the horse is taking regular steps or not.

- Be aware of the 'lift' in the steps. Some horses trot up very flat and others show much more spring in their gait. Be prepared to recognise the stiff, but still forward older horse; the full-of-himself younger horse that won't maintain a rhythm; the older 'pottery' horse; and the horse that is actually lame.

- Look at the levelness of the horse's hips as he moves away from you – the level of both sides of the hindquarters should be the same.

- Study the way the feet make contact with the ground. Is the weight taken evenly over the foot from side to side, or does the horse take more weight on one part of his foot than the other?

- Does the foot pick up, travel forward straight, and set down again, or does it deviate in its 'flight path' between picking up and coming down again?

- Always watch the way the horse leaves the stable and the way he turns during the trot-up. These are two moments when the horse may show you some action traits (such as hock stiffness) which you would not have noticed if you had not been looking.

- Make sure that you can lead a horse effectively and that, if briefing an assistant and the horse is lazy or sharp, you are there to assist if he/she is in trouble. Verbal encouragement from behind may motivate a lazy horse, while some reassuring soothing from the handler will usually settle a sharp horse.

Horse Behaviour

Know how to deal with young, highly spirited or problem horses, including those with stable vices.

ELEMENT

C **10.1.1** Give examples of aspects of equine conduct/maturity that make it unwise to run particular horses with a herd.

S **10.2.1** Explain behaviour and practices designed to gain the horse's confidence in stables.

C **10.3.1** Give examples of stable vices, their consequences and ways of controlling them.

S **10.4.1** Give examples of how discomfort and/or undue stress are shown in the ridden horse's behaviour.

What the examiner is looking for

- It is unlikely that there will be a horse in your exam who exhibits any stable vices and so almost certainly this information will be sought orally.

- You may be asked about horses living in a group situation (permanently at grass) and you should be able to talk about horses that may not be compatible with each other. (Element 10.1.1)

- There may be signs in the stable yard, such as anti-weaving bars, indicating that there are horses in the establishment that weave.

- Chewed wood in stables or on fences can also be a sign that horses have bad habits.

- Be able to discuss any stable habit or repetitive behaviour (e.g. weaving, crib biting, box walking) which might be regarded as a 'vice'. (Elements 10.2.1 and 10.3.1)

- Be able to discuss with the examiner how you might deal with these vices and what methods you might suggest to eliminate or minimise them.

- You may be asked to discuss how you would know that a ridden horse was suffering discomfort or stress. (Element 10.4.1)

How to become competent

- Stable vices or repetitive habits exhibited by the horse would include: weaving, crib biting, windsucking, box walking, banging the stable door, kicking the back of the stable, and tearing rugs.

- You should ideally have seen a horse at some time who demonstrates these patterns of behaviour (but not one horse carrying out all these vices!). If you have not seen all of them, then make sure that you have read about the habits you have not seen displayed and/or ask someone with more experience about them.

- There are different opinions about the causes of vices, and ongoing research is revealing new information which suggests that not all vices are necessarily learned from or copied from another horse.

- Try to stay up to date with current thinking on this issue and ask your vet for his/her opinion.

- Any repetitive behaviour can have a detrimental effect on the horse's well-being and this should be recognised and understood.

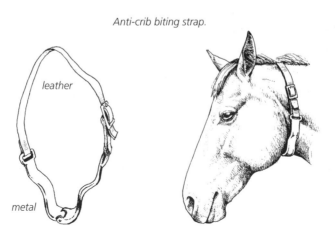

Anti-crib biting strap.

leather

metal

Stable door fitted with anti-weaving bars.

- The more the vice is demonstrated then the more stress the horse is likely to be exhibiting.

- Make sure that you can describe the symptoms for all the vices that are listed above.

- Often vices are initially demonstrated if a horse is bored or not occupied sufficiently. Ideally he should be worked adequately, turned out to graze regularly or stabled in an interesting part of the yard where he has plenty to look at.

- Find out how the different vices might be 'treated', and talk to anyone who can give you first-hand information about dealing with behavioural traits.

- Rarely will horses demonstrate their vice when turned out at grass, although confirmed 'crib biters' will still find a fence to crib on. It is generally regarded as a remedy to turn the horse out as much as possible to give him plenty to occupy him and distract him from his bad habit.

- There are other vice-control measures that you should know about: such as anti-weaving bars (for weaving), or a collar or strap behind the ears and around the gullet (for cribbing and windsucking).

- All behaviour traits demonstrated by the horse (particularly those he exhibits frequently rather than as a one-off reaction) tell you something about the personality of the horse.

- Make sure that you are able to recognise and relate to the nervous horse, the bossy horse, the horse with no manners, and the insecure horse. Learning to recognise a horse's 'personality' comes with practice – through looking after many horses and watching the way they relate to each other and to us.

- Remember that some behaviour patterns relate partly to the horse's natural instincts, while others are patterns that have developed as a learned response from what we do with the horse.

- Be aware that there can often be problems if you turn mares and geldings out together. Some geldings can become territorial and fights may occur, particularly in the spring or summer when the mares may be coming into season.

- It is wiser to turn horses out in groups of the same sex. It is generally better to turn young horses out together as they will interact and amuse themselves, whereas a young male horse that is put into a more established group of older horses may well have to 'fight his corner' to secure his status in the group.

- Be aware of behavioural traits that might demonstrate discomfort or stress when the horse is being ridden.

- The horse cannot verbally tell you of worry or discomfort; he can only show you by the way he behaves.

- Any uncharacteristic behaviour (resistance in the mouth, bucking, running away or just tightness in the back) could indicate that the tack is pinching.

- Development of problems with the teeth or mouth would be shown by resistance to the bit.

- Nervousness or reluctance to go forward past something the horse is genuinely frightened of would again be demonstrated by the horse's lack of compliance.

- Take every opportunity to study a new horse coming into the yard. 'Read' every horse both in the stable and out, and learn to recognise the different traits demonstrated by each individual. This will enable you to become more aware and therefore better equipped to manage the horses in your care.

Horse Health

The candidate should have:

Knowledge of treating minor injuries, minor ailments, sickness and lameness; how to prevent them, and when to call the veterinary surgeon and what information to give.

Know how to administer medicine and implement worming procedures.

ELEMENT

C	**11.1.1**	List the contents of a well-stocked first-aid cabinet for horses.
C	**11.2.1**	Explain cold hosing and the problems you may use it for.
S	**11.2.2**	Explain tubbing and the problems you may use it for.
S	**11.2.3**	Explain poulticing/hot fomentations and the problems you may use them for.
C	**11.3.1**	Give the causes, symptoms and treatment of colic.
S	**11.3.2**	Give the causes, symptoms and treatment of azoturia.
S	**11.3.3**	Give the causes, symptoms and treatment of laminitis.
C	**11.4.1**	Give the principles of sick nursing.
C	**11.4.2**	Explain an isolation procedure and the diseases you may use it for.
C	**11.5.1**	Describe a suitable worming routine.

What the examiner is looking for

- The information in these elements will be sought through oral questions within the practical oral section of the exam.

- Any riding school or equestrian establishment should have a first-aid cabinet, appropriate for treating minor ailments which may arise and need some immediate treatment prior to the possible later visit by a vet. You may be asked for your ideas on what this cabinet should contain. (Element 11.1.1)

- Hosing, tubbing, poulticing and fomentations are all recognised treatments for acute conditions that the horse might suffer from, and the examiner will expect you to have some knowledge and understanding of these. (Elements 11.2.1, 11.2.2 and 11.2.3)

- Hosing is used frequently when acute minor injuries occur, such as the horse coming in from the field with a small wound. Cold water is trickled over the damaged area and the application of continual cold water has a constricting effect on the broken blood vessels, helping to close them and allow the blood to clot; any surface impurities would also be rinsed out by hosing.

- Tubbing would be more appropriate for a foot injury and can be done with hot or cold water. The horse's heel should be greased to prevent chapping or cracking if tubbing is going to be repeated for a few days.

- Poulticing is the application of a substance which maintains heat and therefore has a drawing effect on a wound or area. It encourages blood to the area to assist healing or to draw out infection or a foreign body from a wound.

- Fomenting is the simple application of heat or cold to an area to encourage blood to the area (hot) or constrict blood vessels (cold) to aid healing; alternate hot and cold applications have a proven beneficial effect.

- You will be asked about the causes, symptoms and treatment of colic, azoturia, and laminitis (and other common conditions). These are all serious but usually

Fomenting a forearm.

avoidable conditions which the horse could suffer from, and you must be able to talk clearly about all three. (Elements 11.3.1, 11.3.2 and 11.3.3)

■ Make sure that you have carefully studied (*The BHS Veterinary Manual*) the causes, symptoms and treatment of colic, azoturia and laminitis.

■ You will also be asked to discuss a sick-nursing regime for an ill horse and an isolation procedure for a horse suffering from an infectious or contagious condition. (Elements 11.4.1 and 11.4.2)

■ The two most important criteria to observe for either sick nursing or isolation are: (1) one person only (as far as possible) to look after the horse so that observation is maximised and risk of infection is minimised; and (2) segregation from the main hubbub of the yard so that the horse has peace and quiet and again risk of cross-infection is minimised.

■ You should be able to discuss worming programmes for horses, including the need for good pasture management as part of a policy for good parasite control in the horse. (Element 11.5.1)

■ Be sure that you know what worming programme is adopted in the establishment where you have trained and why this system is used.

How to become competent

■ As your experience develops you will inevitably see horses that are off colour or ill and horses that suffer accident, injury and need some basic first aid and management immediately before deciding whether to call the vet.

■ Be sure that you take every opportunity to be observant of the day-to-day pattern of behaviour of the horses in your care, so that you notice instantly if this 'normal' behaviour changes as this might be an indicator of a developing problem.

■ Symptoms of any condition are always 'abnormal' to the horse's normal pattern of behaviour, so it is essential that you 'know' your horses as well as possible.

■ Be able to identify pain demonstrated by your horse. Pain can be manifested in several ways. In a limb or foot the affected limb may be held up or rested excessively, there may be signs of injury, swelling or abnormal stance with a reduced weight-bearing inclination. The foot or limb may be hot, show signs of swelling (in a limb) and the horse may exhibit pain (flinching, reluctance to bear weight or reaction away from light pressure). If there is pain in the gut (digestive tract) the horse may demonstrate restlessness and be inclined to lie down and get up again, as if trying to find a place of comfort. The horse may be off his food and show increasing distress and sometimes violence.

- Pain associated with colic is within some part of the digestive tract; pain from azoturia will be more associated with tightness over the large muscle mass areas (over the back and throughout the upper part of the hindquarters) with particular emphasis on the muscles of the hind limbs.

- Pain associated with laminitis will almost always be associated with the feet, more often the front feet. The affected feet will be hot (feeling the hoof with the hand and comparing both front feet and then likewise the hind feet, will enable you to compare the heat of all four feet). The horse will demonstrate a reluctance to walk out, and he may be pottery and appearing to 'save himself'.

- Colic can be very scary if you have not seen it before. The horse can become violent if a veterinary surgeon is not called to administer a pain-killer and muscle relaxant. When a vet is treating any of the above mentioned conditions, make quite sure that you watch what is done and ask tactfully at an appropriate moment what the horse is being treated with. Invite the vet to tell you anything else that is relevant to the immediate treatment or after-care.

- Make sure that you have read up thoroughly on colic, laminitis and azoturia. Try to read *Horse and Hound* regularly as this publication tends to be very up to date with the latest methods of treating horses with these conditions and what the possible cost of treatment might be (this will vary greatly from one part of the country to another, but you should know what it is for your area).

- Take every opportunity to watch the vet when he is called out to treat a horse in your yard.

- Be able to discuss what you might keep as essentials in the veterinary medicine cabinet. Remember that the contents will be 'past the sell by date' if not used or serviced, so regular checking and updating of the contents is essential. The basics should include: surgical scissors (blunt ended and possibly slightly curved), dressings (non-stick such as Melolin), and one or two sterile bandages for use only in a medical emergency, a thermometer, some Vaseline (e.g. for greasing heels, lubricating a thermometer before inserting into the rectum, etc.), a basic application for wounds (salve or powder), and a stethoscope. You might include the veterinary surgeon's phone number visibly written on the cabinet. You might also keep your worming doses in the cabinet.

- Be able to discuss a good sick-nursing regime. Be clear that a contagious condition is one that can only be transferred to another horse by physical contact between an infected horse and non-infected horse. This contact may be as the result of the infection being transferred by an intermediary 'conveyor' (e.g. ringworm spores are transferred from one horse to another through contact, via, for example, tack or grooming brushes used on an infected horse and then again on a 'clean' horse).

- Be able to discuss a worming programme appropriate for horses that are stabled or at grass. Worming procedures vary, but all horses can suffer to some degree from infestation by worms (roundworms, small and large redworms, tapeworms and bots).

- Make sure that you understand the way in which worms act as parasites in horses. Worms use the horse as a 'host', from which they derive nutritional benefit while having a debilitating effect on the horse.

- Eradication is the aim through assessment of the worm burden by an egg count, treatment with medication to kill the worms and good pasture management to reduce the worm burden on the grassland. This combined approach should maintain horses in good condition, while managing the pasture to the best of your ability and lowering the likelihood of re-infestation.

- Try to find out what worming programme is in place for the yard where you work or train. Discuss the regime with your yard manager or instructor; ask why the programme is used and what worm doses are used, and when, throughout the year.

- Make sure that you have watched horses being treated with a worm dose in a plastic syringe – the dose being given orally. Be aware of the need to check the syringe being used is 'within date' and is sterile at the outset.

- Make sure that you are aware of the need to record the worming procedure and to dispose of the spent syringe in a safe manner where it could not pose a hazard to any animal or human who accidentally picks it up.

Fittening

Know procedures for preparing and looking after fit horses, and how to prepare horses for the show ring and other competitions.

ELEMENT

C   **12.1.1** Give a suitable period of time for getting a horse fit for a Pony Club one-day event or Riding Club one-day event.

S   **12.1.2** Describe suitable work given during the first 3–4 weeks of an appropriate fittening programme for Pony Club or Riding Club events.

C   **12.1.3** Describe suitable work given during the second 3–4 weeks of an appropriate fittening programme for Pony Club or Riding Club events.

C   **12.1.4** Describe suitable work given during the third 3–4 weeks of an appropriate fittening programme for Pony Club or Riding Club events.

C   **12.2.1** Explain the value of using walking exercise, hills, trot and canter work, short gallops, lungeing.

S   **12.3.1** Explain how a fittening programme may differ for 'show' horses.

S   **12.4.1** Give examples of a routine week that is appropriate for maintaining a horse's fitness level.

What the examiner is looking for

- The questions on fittening will come in the theory section of the examination and you are likely to be asked questions in your group.

- The time you might consider to be appropriate for fittening a horse to Pony Club or Riding Club one-day event level would be in the region of six to eight weeks, assuming that the horse was not starting from a point of no work at all or was restarting after an injury. (Element 12.1.1)

■ You may be asked about the work appropriate to the first 3 or 4 weeks of a fittening programme (Element 12.1.2) but remember this will depend a little on where you start from (see 'How to become competent').

■ You will be expected to discuss the slow development of the horse's work over a period of weeks to show that you understand the gradual build up of work in walk, trot, canter and then some faster canter work to progressively achieve the fitness required. (Elements 12.1.2, 12.1.3, 12.1.4 and 12.2.1)

■ You may be asked about how the fitness of a one-day-event horse may differ from that of a show horse. (Element 12.3.1) You must demonstrate an awareness of the different requirements of work of the event horse and the show horse, and this will be reflected in the type of fitness each requires.

■ You may be asked about work to maintain the level of a horse's fitness and here again you must demonstrate an understanding of the principles of fittening, followed by sustained work to maintain the fitness level. (Element 12.4.1)

How to become competent

■ It is quite easy to study books by leading event riders to help you understand the system or method that they adopt to fitten their horses for competition. This can be interesting but may also be confusing, as riders use slightly differing methods to suit their own circumstances.

■ Be aware that the basic principle of fittening a horse to do anything is to enable him to fulfil the work required of him with no stress to his limbs, wind or mental state, and no resulting damage (the day after or subsequently).

■ There can be no finite time to get a horse fit for a specific job because it will depend on so many criteria. Make sure that you consider the type and age of the horse, how often (or if) he has been fit before, how long (if at all) has he been out of work, whether there is any reason (such as a past injury) which may inhibit your progression of work. The facilities that you have available to you may also affect the way you choose to fitten the horse.

- Make sure that you take every opportunity to speak to riders who get horses fit for different activities.

- Study horses in different disciplines (even watching racehorses on the television) and what they look like as their fitness develops or when they are fit and competing.

- Make sure that you recognise the difference between a horse that is lean, muscled and fit and one that is thin and looking poor.

- Horses involved in any type of galloping work (event horses or racehorses) should always look lean (carrying only enough weight to look sleek and healthy), and not carrying any excess, which would put extra strain on them when they are galloping.

- Show horses, by comparison, are not required to gallop to any great extent and are more likely to carry a fair amount of flesh, which makes them look well rounded and perhaps more 'comfortable' on the eye.

- These days there are some concerns about the excessive weight carried by many show horses and the subsequent strain this is likely to exert on the limbs, heart and wind in the long term. Excess weight is therefore increasingly being regarded as unacceptable.

- Make sure that you are able to talk about the value of walking exercise and steady trot work to develop stamina, and the introduction of canter and more demanding speeds in canter to strengthen the cardio-vascular system.

- Recognise that all three basic paces play an equal part in the fitness development. Walk is vital in the early fittening work. Trot work develops stamina and staying power. Working up and down hills increases the horse's balance, flexibility and sure-footedness. Canter develops the cardio-vascular system of the horse (heart and lungs).

- Lungeing can also be a useful tool in the fittening programme and gives you a chance to watch the basic paces of your horse and to see where he is working – or not, as the case may be.

- Once the horse is fit, consider a maintenance programme. Usually a horse does not need to be continually schooled, cantered, jumped day in and out to keep him fit. The maintenance work must suit the horse and your lifestyle otherwise it will become too much of a chore and you will not be able to follow it.

- With the horses that you ride or are involved in looking after, make sure that you are aware of how fit they are.

- Consider the signs that indicate fitness such as: how much the horse sweats or blows after exertion, how quickly the sweating/blowing recovers when you stop the effort, and how tired the horse seems after work.

- Be able to discuss a fittening programme that either you have worked through yourself, or someone close to you has used and you have been able to follow its success.

- Remember that the success of a fittening programme is dependent on the consistency of the work and the awareness of the rider of any minor problems which might affect the horse's welfare. Be able to check the horse's legs, his enthusiasm, his wind (how well he copes with the increasing fast work), and his recovery.

- Be aware that problems or interruptions in the fitness programme will have an effect on the overall time taken to fitten the horse. If he suffers an injury from which he has to take time to recuperate then this break in the fittening programme must be accounted for. Similarly a very hot period of weather may inhibit how your programme is running.

General Knowledge

Know the risks and responsibilities involved when riding on the public highway. Correct procedures in the event of accidents. Safety rules and fire precautions in the stable yard.

Know about the BHS and its departments.

ELEMENT

C	**13.1.1**	Describe correct procedures when riding in a group on the highway.
C	**13.1.2**	Give examples of correct leading in hand on the road.
C	**13.2.1**	Explain the procedure to be adopted in the event of a fire in stables.
S	**13.3.1**.	Explain what is meant by the term 'risk assessment', and give an example.
S	**13.4.1**	Give examples of the responsibilities of individual BHS departments.
C	**13.4.2**	List the benefits of being a BHS member.
C	**13.5.1**	Describe the action to be taken in the event of an accident involving a rider.

What the examiner is looking for

- Through passing the Riding and Road Safety exam, which is a prerequisite for taking your Stage 2 exam, you will already be familiar with the correct procedure when riding in a group on the road. (Element 13.1.1)

- Make sure that you can discuss when riders should ride in single or double file on the road, how and when to make hand signals and what general measures of awareness are essential for rider safety.

- Be able to discuss clothing for horse and rider on the road.

- Make sure you can talk about how to negotiate junctions and hazards when riding in a group.

- Leading in hand on the road (whether mounted or unmounted) is something with which you should already be familiar. (Element 13.1.2)

- Fire prevention is essential in any stable yard, as is safety to avoid accidents. You may be asked about how to minimise the 'risk' of an accident, and about what you should do in the first instance if involved in an accident. (Elements 13.2.1, 13.3.1 and 13.5.1)

- Be able to discuss the fire protection policy that is in place in your yard. A fire 'drill' should be part of the regular Health and Safety policy in any yard and is an essential part of the induction of new students or members of staff.

- Similarly accident procedure guidelines should be clearly laid down in your establishment and everyone should be aware of the procedure and able to adopt it smoothly in any event. Be able to discuss this procedure clearly if asked by the examiner.

- You will already be a BHS member as this is mandatory if you are taking a BHS examination. (Elements 13.4.1 and 13.4.2) You should therefore be able to discuss the benefits of personal membership.

- Make sure that you are aware of the range of services of the BHS Standards Directorate with regard to its administration of exams and its Register of Instructors, and how the latter assists and supports professional riding instructors.

- Make sure that you have considered the multifaceted role of the BHS and can discuss its many roles in the horse world. (Elements 13.4.1 and 13.4.2)

How to become competent

- If you ride regularly on the road then you should automatically be able to discuss aspects of riding safely in a group.

- If you are not regularly riding on the highway then study *The BHS Riding and Road Safety Manual: Riding and Roadcraft* to remind yourself of good practice.

- Make sure that you study the section on leading on the road, and remind yourself that you should always be between the horse and the traffic, whether you are leading one horse 'in hand' or you are leading another horse from the horse you are riding. Be aware of good practice when riding on bridleways and other permitted routes.

- Discuss 'risk assessments' with your employer or with the trainer in your establishment. Making a structured consideration of the risks involved with various activities in your riding establishment, so as to minimise the possibility of an accident occurring, is what risk assessment is all about. The activity might be for something as simple and regular as 'bringing horses in from the field' or something more seasonal like 'clipping a horse'. Risk assessments are part of any good policy for health and safety in and around the yard.

- As a member of the BHS you should know what the benefits are – they are listed in your member's annual year book. Benefits include third-party insurance for you if you are out and about with your horse and you have an accident; access to a legal help line; being able to take the BHS examinations; contributing to the welfare and safety of horses through training and education; and being part of a voice to influence the provision of access in the countryside,

- Make sure that you have discussed with your instructor exactly what procedure is followed in your establishment in the event of an accident. It is unlikely that you have come thus far in your experience with horses without having been involved in some way in an accident, either falling off a horse yourself or seeing someone else fall off.

- Be confident that you would know how to react in the event of an accident and that this might occur in the riding school (enclosed arena) or out and about while hacking.

- Your basic ability to 'cope' is reliant on your knowledge and common sense.

- Keep calm, reassure anyone who might be injured and go to their aid immediately, enlist any other help available to catch a loose horse, help organise other riders, and call help if required. Remember that after the incident has been dealt with satisfactorily there must always be a full report made in an accident book as soon after the accident as is reasonably possible.

Grassland Care

Know the basic management required to maintain grazing paddocks in suitable condition for horses/ponies living out or on daily turn-out.

ELEMENT

S   **14.1.1** Explain the reasons for harrowing pasture.

S   **14.1.2** Explain the reasons for rolling pasture.

S   **14.1.3** Explain the reasons for fertilising and topping paddocks.

S   **14.1.4** Outline a pasture maintenance regime.

C   **14.2.1** Explain the benefits of grazing horse pasture with sheep and/or cattle.

C   **14.3.1** Give minimum acreage ratios required for horses.

What the examiner is looking for

- This will be examined in the theory session of the exam, so the questions will be oral in discussion.

- You may be asked to describe how pasture might be managed for horses over a period of a year. (Element 14.1.4)

- Through the winter you would probably choose to graze some horses on paddocks that drain the best and are easily accessible, so as to facilitate feeding additional forage through the colder months. Pasture that tends not to drain so well would be rested to avoid unnecessary poaching by the horses.

- Early spring would bring the opportunity to roll and harrow pasture that had been grazed through the winter, possibly reseeding any poached areas and certainly including a period of rest to allow the grass to recuperate.

- Fertilising is another spring activity for fields where a hay crop may be an option. If this is the case, the pasture would be 'shut up' from around spring until the hay was taken in late June/July time.

- Be able to discuss the pros and cons of taking hay from a small acreage: a disadvantage is that often it is difficult to ensure a good quality crop; an advantage is that it can be cheaper to make your own hay.

- Grazing through the spring and summer needs to take account of managing an increased volume of grass, dealing with weeds (which are prolific in the spring and summer) and rotating the pasture to maintain all paddocks in good heart.

- Be able to talk about maintaining fencing in good order, topping pasture if necessary, and management of weeds – especially the eradication of ragwort.

- You may be asked specifically about harrowing, rolling, topping and fertilising and also about cross-grazing the pasture with other animals, such as sheep or cattle. (Elements 14.1.1, 14.1.2, 14.1.3 and 14.2.1)

- In autumn you need to consider the management of the last autumn 'flush' of grass growth, and possibly spreading of farmyard manure if you can access it. You also need to be aware of the possible problems that fallen acorns or apples could cause if you have oak and apple trees on the property.

- You will also be expected to discuss the approximate acreage which would be the minimum acceptable on which to keep a horse. (Element 14.3.1)

- Bear in mind that the principle of one horse/pony per acre is not really appropriate (it would be almost impossible to sustain one pony/horse all year around on only one acre). But as the numbers go up, it is easier to manage the pasture to sustain the number of equines (i.e. four ponies/horses on four acres would be manageable, because paddocks could be set up in rotation).

- The examiner will expect you to be able to discuss the basic management of pasture at any time of the year. It is probably easiest to think of the year month by month in terms of what might be carried out on the land to maintain it, but you must be able to pick up the discussion at any point in the year.

How to become competent

- If you are working in an establishment that has an acreage of land which is used for the horse, be sure to ask about the pasture management and observe the procedures carried out.

- Generally pasture that is used only for horses has some special considerations to take into account. Horses are extremely selective in their grazing habits and if pasture is heavily grazed by horses, it is easy for it to become 'horse-sick'. Horse-sick pasture is identified by areas of apparently 'lawn-like' grazing interspersed with patches of rank long grass where the horses have soiled and then avoided grazing.

- Pasture cross-grazed by sheep or cattle is more likely to be evenly grazed, and the cross-grazing also helps to eradicate the parasite infestation that horse paddocks may be burdened with.

- Make a point of watching how pasture is rolled, harrowed, topped and fertilised. Ask the contractor about the type of fertiliser being used. Study the basic principles of using a natural (organic) fertiliser such as farmyard manure (difficult to get these days because it is too valuable to the farmer for him to spare it for your horses!) as opposed to inorganic fertiliser such as NPK (nitrogen, phosphorus, potassium – potash).

- Understand that harrowing and rolling is done to improve the land in early spring, as soon as the land is dry enough to put machinery onto it (it must be just firm enough to roll, but not hard so that the roller makes little impression).

- In the field maintenance regime remember that picking up droppings or some kind of system for keeping droppings to a minimum will reduce the worm burden on the grassland.

- It will also be necessary to be aware of the need to manage weeds such as docks, thistles and particularly any influx of ragwort.

- When discussing cross-grazing, be able to compare the benefits of sheep over cattle, or vice versa. Sheep are easier to manage but need low fencing (which might involve wire) to contain them, and they take the grass lower than horses can graze. Cattle, however, sweeten the grassland more with their manure and have an eradicating effect on most horse parasites, but they can be damaging to fencing and any jumps that might be in the field and generally are more unruly to manage.

- Be quite clear in your mind of what a year's basic programme of work to maintain pasture would involve.

- Be able to talk about minimum acreage with regard to managing perhaps six acres with six horses/ponies grazing on this land. You would need to be able to discuss a method of splitting up the pasture into at least two and possibly three paddocks, so that at any time you had the horses grazing one paddock while the other two were resting or perhaps being treated for improvement.

- Be able to discuss what you would do with pasture of a designated acreage which had been neglected and become horse-sick, if you had to manage and improve it for twelve months.

Watering and Feeding

Understand the value of grass and concentrates and the significance of carbohydrates, proteins, fats and oils, minerals, vitamins, fibre and water in the horse's diet.

Be able to monitor and organise the feed store.

ELEMENT

C	**15.1.1** Explain why water is vital to the horse.
S	**15.2.1** Describe the importance of carbohydrates in the horse's diet.
S	**15.2.2** Describe the importance of protein in the horse's diet.
S	**15.2.3** Describe the importance of fats and oils in the horse's diet.
S	**15.2.4** Describe the importance of minerals and vitamins in the horse's diet.
C	**15.2.5** Explain why fibre is so important in the horse's diet.
C	**15.2.6** Discuss the meaning of the phrase 'balanced diet' and give an example of a balanced diet for specific types of horse/pony.
C	**15.3.1** Give examples and underlying reasons for adjusting the grass-kept pony/horse's diet through the seasons.
C	**15.4.1** Give examples of quantities of bulk to concentrate ratios for maintenance and for horses in light and medium work.
S	**15.5.1** Explain how to monitor and arrange/store feed stocks.

What the examiner is looking for

- The discussion on feeding will be covered in the theory section of the examination, again in your group of up to five candidates. As with all the theory sessions, listen carefully to the answers other candidates give and be prepared to add to or, if necessary, contradict an answer given by someone else, if you think it is incorrect or you can enhance it with more information.

- You will be asked to discuss the importance of water in the diet. (Element 15.1.1) You must be able to state the function of water (cools the system, is a constituent of blood, urine, sweat and all body fluids, cleanses the system and provides a medium to aid digestion and quench thirst).

- You will be asked about the value of carbohydrates in the diet. Remember these are the energy-giving components of the feed; they are made up of the elements carbon, hydrogen and oxygen. (Element 15.2.1)

- You will also be asked about the role of protein in the diet. Protein is the body-building component of the feed. Proteins are made up of amino acids. (Element 15.2.2) These form the body's 'building blocks'. Make sure that you do not confuse proteins and carbohydrates.

- You may be asked about the role of fats and oils in the diet. These are two and a half times the calorific value of a similar amount of carbohydrate. (Element 15.2.3) Fats and oils help maintain the body temperature, are a source of storage for the body (too much carbohydrate is converted into fat for storage and can be reconverted back to provide a fuel source if the horse is not fed enough carbohydrate).

- You may be asked about vitamins and minerals and their value to the horse. Be clear that these act as catalysts to activate or assist in chemical changes in the body. They act as essential balancers or facilitators to allow the other systems of digestion to operate smoothly. (Element 15.2.4)

- Be able to discuss the importance of fibre in the diet. (Element 15.2.5) Because the horse is a browsing herbivore that is dependent on keeping his lengthy digestive system at least half full for much of the time, he is admirably designed to live exclusively on grass. Being subjected to stabling does not lend itself to improving the efficient and smooth running of the digestive system. Maintaining a regular intake of fibre allows the horse's digestive system to work as closely as possible to the way it would in its natural state. Fibre assists in the active passage of food through the digestive tract. Fibre is digested in the hind gut with the help of bacteria (gut flora).

- You will be asked to discuss what is meant by a 'balanced diet'. (Element 15.2.6)

- You should be able to explain that a balanced diet provides the horse with all the nutrients he requires for his lifestyle and in appropriate amounts relative to each other, thus providing a ration which maintains him in an optimum state of health. Usually this would be provided by water, hay or haylage and perhaps a small amount of some concentrate food with possible access to grass.

- You must be able to discuss why it might be necessary to adjust a horse/pony's diet according to the season and how he is kept (at grass). (Element 15.3.1)

- You will also be asked about the amounts of food and ratios of feed you might use for horses in light or medium work or to maintain a level of work. (Element 15.4.1) Unless the examiner states what work the horse is doing then ask or create a scenario yourself. It is pointless to estimate amounts of food if you do not know: the size of the horse, the age of the horse, the temperament and type of horse, what work it is doing and perhaps how competent its rider is (and whether it is stabled or at grass).

- You must be able to confidently discuss rations for a horse in your care that does not have access to grass (other than for a brief period of turn-out). In this case he would be dependent on you for all his nutritional needs, and the first consideration must always be the forage ration (in most instances hay or haylage). The forage ration should be at least 50% of the diet. If we consider a horse in medium work, the forage ration would be around 70–75% of the ration. If the horse was around 16hh and weighed 500 kg (1100 lbs) he would eat between 13–15kg (28–32 lbs) of food per day (2.5% of body weight). He would therefore be given around 9–11 kg (19–23 lbs) of forage a day, with the balance being made up of concentrate. So 4–6kg (9–13 lbs) would be concentrate, and this could be split into two or three feeds per day.

- You are likely to be asked how to organise your feed store/room. (Element 15.5.1) Consider the ideal in terms of size appropriate to the number of horses, vermin-proof feed bins, shelves for drying feed bowls, a shelf for supplements or additives, a wipe-clean feed chart, easy to clean floor, a power source (to boil a kettle, if needed), good light source and perhaps room to lay out feed bowls.

How to become competent

- Feeding is an art; it comes with experience of looking at horses' condition, understanding what work they are doing and how well they are doing it, and then feeding them accordingly.

- You will find through practical experience that 'hands on' feeding often bears little relation to the rations recommended 'by the book' or by the feed companies, and this is why it is vital to develop an 'eye' for the look of a horse and a 'feel' when you ride him or teach riders on him. It is through this 'feel' that you learn to be able to adapt rations to the horse's individual needs.

- You must, however, understand the concept of how these 'amounts' are calculated so you know where to start with a horse that you don't know.

- The skill of feeding is somewhat reduced these days because there are so many pre-mixed feeds on the market designed to provide nutrients for every type of equestrian activity (e.g. stud cubes for breeding horses, and competition mixes for different disciplines).

- It is still important that you understand what components go into the feeds and what role their nutrients play in the body functions of the horse.

- Read up on feeding as a subject, then study as many different manufactured feeds and their ingredients as you can.

- Collect literature from major feed companies (e.g. Spillers, or Dodson and Horrell). Most food manufacturers produce comprehensive brochures describing the contents and value to the horse of their feeds.

- Talk to your yard manager about what the horses in 'your' yard are fed and why.

- Learn to recognise when a feed may need to be changed. For example, if the level of the horse's work is changed; if the horse suffers an injury and has to be rested from work; if the weather changes and makes greater demands on the horse's stamina, old and young horses may need slightly different management.

- Make sure you understand the concept of the ratio of bulk to concentrate feed and ensure that the horse's diet is always at least 50% bulk. For horses in medium work the ratio of bulk to concentrate is likely to be between 80% and 60% bulk to 20% and 40% concentrate respectively.

- Make sure that you have looked at the feed chart in your yard and you know exactly what all the horses are fed and why. Consider the work they are doing and the ratio of bulk to concentrate that they receive.

- At every opportunity be prepared to ask about horses' rations: what they are fed, why they have what they have, what work they are doing and what the feed offers in terms of food value.

Stage 3
Riding

Syllabus

Candidates should show a feel for their horses and have an appreciation of any weakness. They should begin to school the horses and to ride them according to their needs.

Candidates who are considered to be below the standard may be asked to retire.

IMPORTANT: Candidates are advised to check that they are working from the latest examination syllabus, as examination content and procedure are liable to alteration. Contact the BHS Examinations Office for up-to-date information regarding the syllabus.

British Horse Society – Stage 3 Syllabus

Stage 3 – Horse Knowledge and Riding
Candidates should show a feel for their horses and have an appreciation of any weakness. They should begin to school the horses and to ride them according to their needs.
Candidates who are considered to be below the standard may be asked to retire.

Unit code number S3RIDI		RIDING	
Learning Outcomes	**Element**	**Assessment Criteria**	
The candidate should be able to:		The candidate has achieved this outcome because s/he can:	**Influence**
Ride effectively yet sympathetically, while maintaining a balanced, correct and supple seat at all gaits.	1.1.1	Give and receive a leg-up	Compulsory
	1.1.2	Demonstrate fluent co-ordinated aid application	Compulsory
	1.2.1	Show poise, balance and the ability to absorb and follow the horse's movement in all three gaits	Supporting
	1.2.2	Show an ability to ride horses forward to a receiving hand	Compulsory
Apply correct influences and smooth application of the aids with a clear understanding of the reasons for them.	2.1.1	Show fluent school figures while maintaining the horse in good form	Supporting
	2.2.1	Show awareness of the horse's response to the aids	Compulsory
Ride horses forward in good form through transitions, turns on the forehand, leg-yielding and the rein back (2 or 3 steps), and, if appropriate, show lengthening and shortening of strides at all gaits.	3.1.1	Show preparation of the horse for transitions and school figures	Compulsory
	3.1.2	Exercise to increase the horse's obedience and suppleness	Compulsory
	3.1.3	Demonstrate planning of work	Compulsory
	3.2.1	Show an awareness of satisfactory work	Supporting
Ride with or without stirrups and with reins in one or both hands.	4.1.1	Show an ability to ride the horse in good form throughout, seat independent of the reins and stirrups	Supporting
Understand the value of school work in the mental, muscular and gymnastic development of the horse.	5.1.1	Describe the horse's basic way of going	Compulsory
	5.2.1	Explain the basic principles of training	Supporting
Ride and jump out of doors over a variety of fences and terrain.	6.1.1	Demonstrate a balanced, secure position suitable for riding over undulating ground and a course of fences	Compulsory
	6.2.1	Demonstrate appreciation of terrain and ground conditions	Compulsory
Ride effectively yet sympathetically, while maintaining a balanced, correct and supple position at all gaits when jumping a grid of fences.	7.1.1	Show a balanced jumping position with a secure lower leg	Compulsory
	7.1.2	Show fluency through the phases of the jump allowing the horse freedom over the fences	Supporting
	7.2.1	Show good approaches with regard for rhythm and pace	Compulsory
Have practical and theoretical knowledge of methods and precautions when getting horses fit for regular work and for novice competitions.	8.1.1	Demonstrate suitable preparation (warm-up) of a horse for jumping with regard for weather and ground conditions	Compulsory
	8.1.2	Care of the horse after exertion with regard for weather conditions	Supporting
Ride effectively yet sympathetically over show jumps up to 1m (3' 3") while maintaining a balanced, correct and supple seat at all gaits.	9.1.1	Show an effective, positive manner in performance	Compulsory
	9.2.1	Show a balanced position from a secure lower leg	Compulsory
	9.2.2	Show fluency through the phases of the jump, allowing the horse freedom over the fences	Supporting
	9.3.1	Demonstrate appreciation of rhythm and pace when jumping a course of show jumps	Compulsory
	9.4.1	Demonstrate suitable corrections when dealing with refusals or run-outs	Supporting
Have knowledge of the rules for riding at competitive and social events.	10.1.1	Explain rules for working in at competitive events	Supporting
	10.2.1	Explain basic principles of welfare for the horse at competitions	Supporting

Unit code number S3RIDI		RIDING	
Learning Outcomes	**Element**	**Assessment Criteria**	
The candidate should be able to:		The candidate has achieved this outcome because s/he can:	**Influence**
Ride effectively yet sympathetically over cross-country fences up to 0.91m (3' 0"), while maintaining a balanced, correct and supple seat at all gaits.	11.1.1	Show an effective, positive manner in performance	Compulsory
	11.2.1	Show a balanced position from a secure lower leg	Compulsory
	11.2.2	Show fluency through the phases of the jump allowing the horse freedom over the fences	Supporting
	11.3.1	Demonstrate appreciation of rhythm and pace when jumping a course of cross-country fences	Compulsory
	11.3.2	Show appreciation of speed with regard for terrain, balance, ground conditions and fence type	Compulsory
	11.4.1	Show appropriate methods of approach for a variety of fence types	Supporting
	11.5.1	Demonstrate suitable corrections if having to deal with refusals or run-outs	Supporting

About the Riding Examination

By the time you reach this level, your basic riding position should be established and secure and you should be seeking to develop greater depth and effectiveness through the regular daily riding of as many different horses as possible.

Working without stirrups on a regular basis will help to deepen your seat and develop suppleness, greater feel and coordination of the aids. You must fully understand the aids you are using to create forward movement through the horse's basic gaits. You must be able to have a positive influence on the horses that you ride, being able to maintain their level of work and show an ability to ride them effectively between the leg and hand, if their level of training and cooperation allows this.

In the section devoted to riding horses on the flat, you will ride two horses, and on at least one of these must show an ability to ride competently without your stirrups in all three basic gaits. On both horses you should demonstrate an ability to find rhythm and harmony with the horse in a relatively short period of time, showing some ability to adapt to find the effect that achieves the feel for that horse. The horses should be sufficiently educated that they will work into a round connection between hand and leg in snaffle bridles. They should be able to work through the basic gaits, through loops, serpentines and circles and show simple exercises such as turn on the forehand, leg yielding and shortening and lengthening of stride in all three paces. You must be able to relate to the strengths and weaknesses in the horses you ride, both in your practical demonstration of riding ability and in discussion.

SUGGESTED COURSE PLANS FOR THE JUMPING SECTION OF STAGE 3

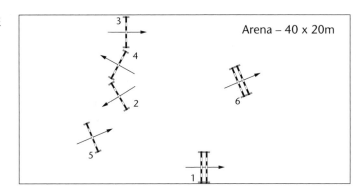

Arena – 40 x 20m

NOTES
- Feet interlocked on fences 2, 3 and 4.
- Fences 5–6 related distance
- RH wing of fence 5 in line with LH wing of fence 1

Arena – 60 x 20m

NOTES
- LH wing fence 1 is 2m (6ft 6ins) in from outside wall
- Fence 2 minimum of 15m (50ft) from end of school
- Fences 2 and 5 and 4 and 7, wings interlocked
- Double is kinder on candidates if 2 strides, with upright coming out
- Fences 4–5 related distance

In the jumping section you will again ride two horses: one over show jumps and one over cross-country fences. You must demonstrate confidence and competence to ride with security and effect over a small course of fences on trained horses. In the show-jumping work, the jumping will develop over a

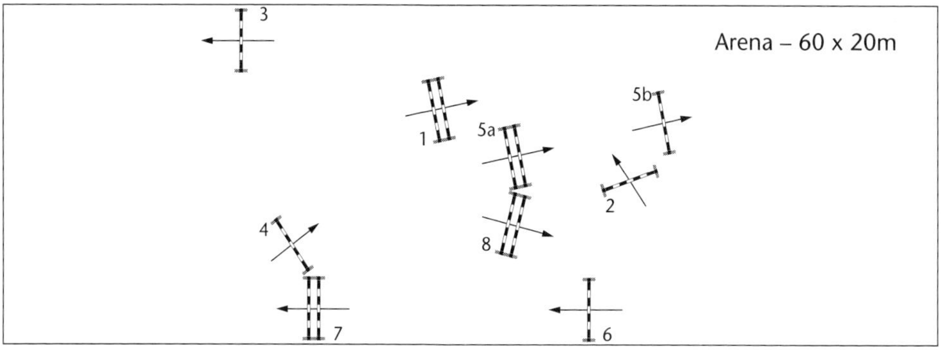

3
Arena – 60 x 20m
5b
1
5a
2
4
8
7
6

NOTES

- Put diagonal fences in first when building
- 4–5a related distance (4,5 strides)
- 6–7 related distance (4,5 strides)
- No fence closer than 15m (50ft) from end of school
- RH wing of fence 1 in line with LH wing of fence 5a
- Wings 5a and 8 interlocked, as fences 4 and 7

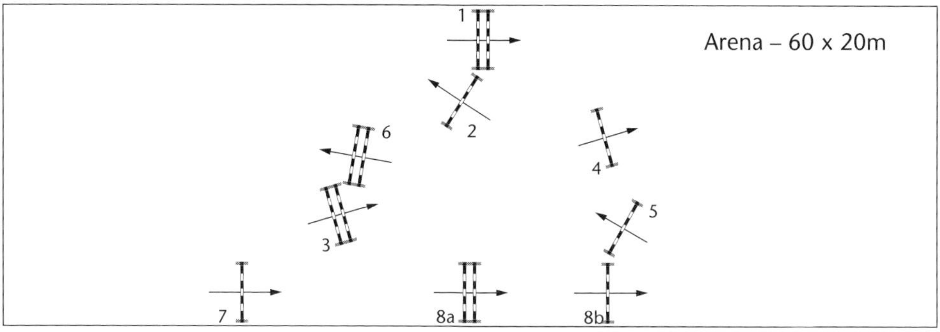

1
Arena – 60 x 20m
6
2
4
5
3
7
8a
8b

NOTES

- Fence 7–8a, 3 strides
- 8a–8b, 1 stride
- 5–6 related distance, 4/5 strides
- 3–4 related distance, 5 strides

progressive grid of fences and will culminate in jumping a numbered course (see above for suggested course plans). In the cross-country section you will ride a second horse over a short course of straightforward schooling-type fixed obstacles, where you should demonstrate a pace appropriate to cross-country riding while taking into account the ground conditions.

The riding at Stage 3 level should demonstrate an evolving competence and confidence in your own ability and the basic initiative to be in control of all situations on trained horses, which may have the ability and enthusiasm to show a little more individuality and need for authority from the rider than the horses presented for riding at Stage 2.

The candidate should be able to:

Ride effectively yet sympathetically, while maintaining a balanced, correct and supple seat at all gaits.

ELEMENT

| C | **1.1.1** Give and receive a leg-up. |

| C | **1.1.2** Demonstrate fluent co-ordinated aid application. |

| S | **1.2.1** Show poise, balance and the ability to absorb and follow the horse's movement in all three gaits. |

| C | **1.2.2** Show an ability to ride horses forward to a receiving hand. |

What the examiner is looking for

- You will be expected to give and receive a leg-up to another candidate, probably when you change horses after your first ride. (Element 1.1.1)

- Make sure you put your whip down. Bear in mind that you will probably not know the person you are legging up so the instructions between you must be clear. Often a poor leg-up occurs because the two people involved are not co-ordinated and one pushes when the other is not ready. If you are used to giving or receiving a leg-up on a count of three, then it is essential that only one person does the counting! If you both count together you can be sure that one of you will be out of sync. Suggest to the person receiving the leg-up that he counts and you will push on 'three'. Similarly when you are being given the leg-up, tell the person throwing you up that you will count and they are to push as you count 'three' because that is when you will spring.

- The whole essence of a leg-up is that the rider is given an additional boost to his spring, to put him up onto the horse. Thus the 'spring' is essential.

- The ability to give and receive a leg-up is important at this level because there may be instances (such as dealing with a young horse or remounting a rider with short stirrups) when this is the most practical and efficient way of remounting a rider.

Correct basic riding position.

- You must demonstrate a practical competence to both give and receive a leg-up to a standard which would be safe in any given situation. It must not end up as a struggle with the rider clambering onto the horse's back.

- The following elements – 1.1.2, 1.2.1 and 1.2.2 – require that you demonstrate your basic position and security at this level, and from that basic position the ability to ride horses forward, influencing them with clear and consistent aids.

- Your position should be well established, with good balance and poise. Your balance should stem from sitting evenly in the saddle with the weight over both seat bones; an imaginary line from your ear, through the shoulder, the hip and into the heel, and another, running from the elbow through the wrist to the horse's mouth, should be clear.

- This balance and consistency in position should be maintained as you absorb and follow the horse's movement, thus demonstrating suppleness and an awareness of how the horse is moving under you.

- As a result of a secure position and a clear understanding of aid application you should be able to ride the horses forward to a receiving hand. (Element 1.2.2) At this level your position must be sufficiently deep and balanced for your aids to be applied with clarity, independence and effect. (Element 1.1.2)

- This section is the underpinning foundation for the whole of your riding and as such is vitally important at this level. Do not underestimate the standard required.

- You will be expected to demonstrate your basic balance, suppleness and effect in all three paces on at least one of the horses you ride.

- In the exam (as at any time) your work without stirrups should deepen and relax you, making you more at one with the horse and allowing you to develop your partnership with the horse more effectively.

How to become competent

- In your training you should be riding without stirrups almost every day or at least every time you ride on the flat.

- It cannot be stressed too highly that riding without stirrups consistently improves your depth and security probably more effectively than any other form of work.

- Be passionate about your position. Be determined to improve it and develop it to be deeper, more supple, more co-ordinated and more effective every time you ride.

- You cannot ride enough different horses – they can all teach you something a little different. Learn to 'read' them before you get on and 'feel' them once you are riding.

- Work on your poise and balance as well as your effectiveness.

- Consider the aids you are trying to give and constantly be aware of the response that each horse gives you.

- Be aware of the importance of good preparation and consistency in the aids that you are using.

- When a horse apparently does not respond, think through your preparation and the aids you gave, consider your effect and whether reinforcement via the whip is appropriate.

- Learn to experiment; find out what works and what causes resistance and loss of

Horse and rider in balance and harmony. Horse working in a soft, round form, accepting the rider's aids.

Loss of harmony. Horse showing resistance and hollowness; rider showing tension and stiffness in position.

Horse dropping behind the contact, overbent with nose behind the vertical and poll too low.

harmony; learn to be effective; some horses need very positive aids, others need a much lighter approach.

- All horses need consistent information, which they must have from consistent thinking and aid application from you.

- Make quite sure that you understand what 'forward' really means. Forward is activity with rhythm and balance and harmony; forward is not running along out of balance, associated with tension and lack of suppleness in the horse.

- Practise giving and receiving a leg-up. Watch those who work in the racing industry to see a leg-up given well. It depends on co-ordination between the person giving the leg-up and rider. It has nothing to do with the strength of the person on the ground and everything to do with lightness, spring and co-ordination between the two involved.

- If you have to count to give a leg up, make quite sure that the timing between you is immaculate and the rider does 'spring'.

- This section needs a fundamental consistency and must be very established and secure at this level. It is the mainstay of much of the rest of the work to be demonstrated as a Stage 3 rider.

The candidate should be able to:

Apply correct influences and smooth application of the aids with a clear understanding of the reasons for them.

ELEMENT

S **2.1.1** Show fluent school figures while maintaining the horse in good form.

C **2.2.1** Show awareness of the horse's response to the aids.

What the examiner is looking for

- These elements will relate to much of the riding of both horses on the flat.

- You will ride two horses in an approximately 50-minute period and there will be up to five of you riding at the same time. The work is directed only generally, in that you will be asked to work to establish a good rhythm and balance in all three gaits. It is then up to you to choose work that is appropriate to the horse you are riding while working the horse in walk, trot and canter in your own time.

- You must demonstrate a clear programme of work that is appropriate for developing rhythm and suppleness.

- You should therefore be showing some large circles, loops and serpentines all of which are clear in what they are meant to be (size and shape).

- You should demonstrate clear preparation for all your work, showing smooth transitions from one pace to another and also within the paces (shortening and lengthening the trot and canter, and not forgetting the walk).

- At any time the examiner should be able to look at you and recognise what you are trying to do and what figure you might be riding.

- Everything about your riding should look well prepared and planned, and nothing should look hurried or hastily decided.

- You should always look as if you are riding in your own designated space with no one around you. This indicates a clear awareness of other riders and where they are going, while you are always planning to stay in a space to give your horse the best possible area in which to work.

- There is no harm in giving a horse a short, sharp reminder with a schooling whip if he constantly ignores your aid – in fact, the examiner would prefer to see you using judgement according to the way the horse is going.

- It is essential that you feel what is going on under you and 'read' the situation so that your response and choice of how best to influence the horse is well considered and effective.

How to become competent

- Confidence in your own ability is absolutely essential. (The examiners do not want to see arrogance, but confidence based on competence and self-belief.)

- You cannot ride too many horses to teach you and upgrade your awareness and effect.

- Training is vital, but try not to learn only during your training sessions or you can become over-dependent on your instructor and rely on him giving you the competence and taking responsibility for 'getting it right'.

- Try to ride 'out and about' as well as in the school. This will teach you to act on your own initiative and find out what works and what doesn't. If you are being run away with in a wide-open space you soon learn to 'take control'! Similarly, if you are out in the countryside and your friends have all jumped a small ditch and your horse is lacking a bit of courage, you will soon learn to 'kick and hold the mane', or encourage him in some other way to be a bit braver and go on. You will learn from these experiences and be a better rider for them.

- Make sure that you are quite clear on the 'floor plan' of the regular school movements used on a daily basis. Circles of 20m, 15m and 10m should all be recognisable, as should 5m loops, three- and four-loop serpentines, turns across the school, and use of the short and long diagonals.

- Maintaining the horse 'in good form' relates to your ability to show the horse working in a good rhythm (regularity) in all three gaits. Also evident should be a consistent connection between the leg and hand and harmony between you and the horse. The horse should show a bend in the direction in which he is going, and you should constantly be able to demonstrate a desire to achieve some suppleness through turns, corners and circles even on the 'stiff side'.

The candidate should be able to:

Ride horses forward in good form through transitions, turns on the forehand, leg-yielding and the rein-back (two or three steps), and, if appropriate, show lengthening and shortening of strides at all gaits.

ELEMENT

| C | **3.1.1** Show preparation of the horse for transitions and school figures. |

| C | **3.1.2** Exercise to increase the horse's obedience and suppleness. |

| C | **3.1.3** Demonstrate planning of work. |

| S | **3.2.1** Show an awareness of satisfactory work. |

What the examiner is looking for

- This work is a continuation of the first two elements and will follow through into subsequent work on the flat.

- All the elements in this section continue to demonstrate your competence at this level.

- All the work you show – transitions and school figures – should show clear preparation and execution. (Elements 3.1.1, 3.1.3 and 3.2.1)

- You will be given minimal direction as to what to do in your riding of the horses, but your competence at this level should enable you to choose work that will increase the horses' obedience and suppleness. (Element 3.1.2)

- You should show an awareness of work that is satisfactory (Element 3.2.1) by rewarding the horse (pat on the neck) after some work you are pleased with, and move on as a result of the satisfactory work to something more demanding. (For example, if 20m circles are good then move on to 15m and then to 10m; or if a turn on the forehand is good, move on to leg-yield.)

- Similarly, if during a turn on the forehand the horse is resistant or walks out half way through, show an awareness by going back to try to improve the result.

- Planning is essential and should be evident. (For example, starting with a 10m circle when the horse is not forward or supple would demonstrate a lack of awareness and planning. Likewise, starting in canter before the horse is settled and rhythmical in walk and trot is probably unwise.)

- The work should show a smooth progression through circles, turns and transitions, using turns on the forehand to see if the horse understands about moving away from the leg. Make a clear demonstration of understanding how to ride a turn on the forehand (from halt) and a turn about the forehand (from walk). In both cases show the correct position, staying over the centre of the horse and apply clear and co-ordinated aids (slight flexion, inside leg behind the girth to move the hindquarters around, outside leg keeping the horse forward and stopping him from trying to step backwards, outside rein preventing the horse from moving forwards and controlling the degree of neck bend). (*Note: Always, 'inside' refers to the way in which the horse is bending – e.g. if bent to the right, the inside leg and inside rein are the right rein and leg.*)

- Once you have discovered how the horse responds to your leg by riding some turns on the forehand then progressing to some leg-yielding would be appropriate. You must demonstrate an awareness of the movement by keeping the horse straight (apart from very slight flexion away from the direction of movement) and then moving the horse forwards and sideways away from your inside leg. The horse's inside hind leg should step more under his body to carry him forwards and sideways without him falling out through the outside shoulder. Co-ordination of your aids is essential here, with your outside leg keeping the horse forward while your inside leg moves the horse sideways; the inside rein maintains the flexion while the outside rein regulates the pace and controls the amount of flexion in the neck. Rhythm is always still a priority.

- Rein-back may also be requested, with you showing a feel for asking the horse to move backwards from a balanced halt. A feel for riding two or three steps and then moving forward again, rewarding the horse, is important. You should show an awareness of when the horse is able to move back with a supple back, in a submissive connection between leg and hand, and when he is hollow in the back and inclined to resist the aids.

How to become competent

- Much of what has already been said in Elements 1 and 2 of the riding section applies here as well and will have reference to Elements 4 and 5.

- There is no substitute for riding as many different horses as possible to develop your feel and awareness of the way in which horses respond to your aids.

- Make sure that you receive plenty of sound instruction on how to ride the developing work; be aware of turn on the forehand, leg-yielding and rein-back in terms of complete understanding of what the movements are, how the horse moves through them and what aids you should be using to effect the correct response.

- Ride these movements often within your pattern of work so that they become very familiar to you and you do not have to think what aids you are using – they come automatically. Once you are not having to think the aids through then you can begin to concentrate more on the preparation and feeling of what is happening underneath you.

- Watch videos of horses performing movements correctly so that you are familiar with what they look like when carried out well. Sit in with a dressage judge, if you have the chance, so that you can watch riders riding movements and listen to the comments made about the quality of the movements. This will also give you an insight into the way a rider prepares for the exercise and the quality of the work that is being presented.

The candidate should be able to:

Ride with or without stirrups and with the reins in one or both hands.

ELEMENT

S **4.1.1** Show an ability to ride the horse in good form throughout, seat independent of the reins and stirrups.

What the examiner is looking for

■ At some stage during the riding of either the first or the second horse you will be asked to include some work without your stirrups in all three paces.

■ If you gain some benefit from riding without your stirrups then it might help you to quit your stirrups early in the session, which then should help you to relax and deepen your seat to assist your subsequent work.

■ When riding without your stirrups you should be able to assume a depth and suppleness that indicates a complete independence from the rein.

■ You may also be asked to ride an exercise, such as a change of rein, with the reins in one hand. This would usually be in trot, and again the examiner is looking for relaxation and independence from the rein.

■ Throughout the riding on the flat be aware of your balance and straightness, make sure that your stirrups are level and use the mirrors (if there are any in the school) to check on your poise, straightness and suppleness.

■ At this level you should be able to help yourself by riding the horses to best effect and monitoring your own performance continually.

■ The examiner is looking for the complete independence of your seat from any reliance on the reins in all three gaits.

How to become competent

■ Ride, ride and ride some more! There is no short cut to developing depth and security. It comes through riding as many different horses as you can, with and without your stirrups, under instruction and independently.

■ Riding out and about, hacking, jumping, and any riding to develop depth and competence will be of benefit in the long term.

■ You must try to ride horses that develop your feel for a supple and active way of going – horses that work confidently between hand and leg and are able to respond with obedience and consistency to the aids.

■ Make sure that you ride often without your stirrups; and riding bareback will also further develop your balance and feel for the horse.

- If you can be lunged regularly on a fairly active horse then this will also develop your independent seat and allow you time to think about your position and balance.

- Exercises on the lunge will improve your suppleness and balance.

The candidate should be able to:

Understand the value of school work in the mental, muscular and gymnastic development of the horse.

ELEMENT

| C | **5.1.1** Describe the horse's basic way of going. |

| S | **5.2.1** Explain the basic principles of training. |

What the examiner is looking for

- At the end of riding either one or both horses you will be asked about the horse and what you have found out about his way of going. (Element 5.1.1)

- What you say about the horse must show clearly that you understand how a horse should be trained and the basic principles of training. (Element 5.2.1)

- Your comments about the horse should reflect your ability to assess the rhythm, suppleness and forwardness of the horse.

- You should be able to recognise whether or not the horse worked from activity in the hind legs, over a supple back and neck, into a submissive connection in the rein.

- From rhythm, suppleness and connection, you would be able to assess how straight the horse is and how much energy is forthcoming.

- Talk about whether or not the horse has a stiffer side, and a soft or hollow side. This relates to the horse's ease of bending on one rein and more reluctance to bend on the other rein.

- On the soft side it is necessary to limit the natural desire of the horse to bend only through his neck and then fall out through the outside shoulder, thus avoiding the energy coming through a 'straight' body to the rein.

- On the stiff side, where the horse is reluctant to bend and maintain activity with the inside hind leg stepping sufficiently under his body, there is then a tendency for him to tip his head to the outside, so avoiding the bend.

- Be able to talk systematically about the horse – avoid jumping from one trait to another.

- Every horse has something in its favour, so get into the habit of bringing out the positive before discussing the negative aspects of the work. For example: 'The horse was quite amenable and obedient, but was a little stiff to the left and reluctant to really go forward from my leg aids,' sounds very different to: 'The horse was stiff and lazy and I didn't like him.'

- Your comments about the horse(s) must apply to the horse(s) that you have actually ridden; they should not be just a stereotyped description which could apply to any horse.

How to become competent

- There are many good books available on training horses; read as much as you can to consolidate your theoretical knowledge.

- Sit in with a dressage judge so that you can watch horses working at Novice and Elementary level to help you understand the quality of good movement and become familiar with terms such as rhythm, suppleness, submission and impulsion and where they apply to the horse's way of going.

- Make sure that you discuss with your instructor the way of going of the horses you ride so that you develop greater understanding of what the horse is doing underneath you.

- Practise talking about horses that you ride so that you are familiar with assessing them in a practical, systematic way.

The candidate should be able to:

Ride and jump out of doors over a variety of fences and terrain.

ELEMENT

C   **6.1.1** Demonstrate a balanced, secure position suitable for riding over undulating ground and a course of fences.

C   **6.2.1** Demonstrate appreciation of terrain and ground conditions.

What the examiner is looking for

- In the jumping section of the exam you will ride two horses: one over show jumps and the other over cross-country fences.

- In the jumping part of the exam you will be required to show a secure and balanced position which will sustain you to ride the horse in harmony over undulating ground and around show jumps and cross-country fences. (Element 6.1.1)

- The show jumping may be on grass or it may be on an artificial surface. The cross-country jumping will, of course, be on grass. In every situation you must be able to judge the ground underneath you and choose the gait and speed according to the 'going'. This will ensure a balanced ride. (Element 6.2.1)

- In the cross-country phase you should be able to show an increased pace appropriate to cross-country riding, if the ground conditions allow it.

- The show jumping will be built up progressively through a grid of fences, and then you will be required to jump a course of show jumps at approximately 1m height (3ft 3in).

- Across country you will be required to jump a course of five to ten straightforward fixed obstacles, which may involve some variations in gradient and terrain.

- Throughout this section your balance and harmony with the horse must be consistent, emanating from a well-established confident jumping position.

- You must demonstrate confidence, independence and initiative in your jumping ability.

How to become competent

- Jump, jump and jump some more! There is no substitute for practice.

- Just as with your position for riding on the flat, your jumping position needs much practice to consolidate your balance, security and confidence.

- Ride lots of horses that jump genuinely – maintaining a good rhythm and balance to a fence and then jumping fluently when they get there.

- Jump gymnastic exercises without your stirrups to develop feel and balance and improve your security and effect.

- If you are able to do any competitive jumping then this is useful.

- Clear-round jumping at a local competition and perhaps some cross-country schooling, will all help you to develop an independence in your jumping.

The candidate should be able to:

Ride effectively yet sympathetically, while maintaining a balanced, correct and supple position at all gaits when jumping a grid of fences.

ELEMENT

C **7.1.1** Show a balanced jumping position with a secure lower leg.

S **7.1.2** Show fluency through the phases of the jump allowing the horse freedom over the fences.

C **7.2.1** Show good approaches with regard for rhythm and pace.

What the examiner is looking for

- As discussed in Element 6 of the ridden section, the foundation for jumping well, in balance and harmony with the horse, is a good basic jumping position.

- The jumping position depends on balance, and the security of a jumping position comes from the lower leg. If the lower leg slips forward, the rider's upper body will tip back out of balance; and if the rider's lower leg slips back; the upper body will tip forward and the balance will be lost. (Element 7.1.1)

- The grid will be built up from a cross-pole, probably with a placing pole from a trot approach. After jumping this once or twice, a second fence will be introduced at one non-jumping stride distance from the first. The approach will still be from trot.

- On each occasion it is important that you ride a well-planned line of approach with a straight line to the centre of the first fence, maintaining rhythm and impulsion in the approach. (Element 7.2.1)

- As the grid develops you will be invited to jump it several times until you are comfortable with the rhythm and pace for your approach. (Element 7.2.1)

- A third fence will be built either one or two non-jumping strides from the second fence, and again the initial approach will still be made in trot.

- Throughout the grid work you should show a fluency in your jumping position, with your balance and security of position allowing you to sustain an allowing hand to the horse over the fences.

How to become competent

- No apology is made for repeating the word practice again and again, because there is no substitute for practice. It is the only way that you will ultimately achieve competence.

- As much grid work as possible will help you to develop a feel for the horse's stride and balance.

- Learn to feel how varying the energy in the approach can affect the feel through the grid.

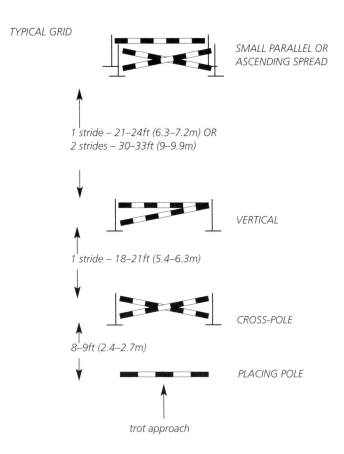

TYPICAL GRID

SMALL PARALLEL OR ASCENDING SPREAD

1 stride – 21–24ft (6.3–7.2m) OR
2 strides – 30–33ft (9–9.9m)

VERTICAL

1 stride – 18–21ft (5.4–6.3m)

CROSS-POLE

8–9ft (2.4–2.7m)

PLACING POLE

trot approach

- When distances are measured exactly between fences to produce a specific number of strides (in this case one and then two) there can be some difference in the feel of fluency over those fences, depending on the speed or energy in the approach.

- If the horse rushes into the placing pole, hurrying over it and bounding into canter, the first distance (which is measured to be taken from a calm trot approach) will feel short and tight.

- If the horse then continues to rush, the next distance will also feel short and tense.

- It is important that you learn to feel the speed of the pace of approach and be able to adapt it if necessary. If the horse is lazy and inactive then you must be able to influence it for greater energy and activity.

- Similarly if the horse is hurried and rushing then a slower pace in the approach or a shorter approach may help to address the problem.

- Some jumping work down a controlled grid without your stirrups, on an obedient horse that you have jumped several times before, will help develop your security and independence.

- Some jumping work down a controlled grid without your reins (knot them on the neck for easy access, if required), on an obedient horse that you have jumped several times before, will help to develop your feel, fluency and independence.

The candidate should:

Have practical and theoretical knowledge of methods and precautions when getting horses fit for regular work and for novice competitions.

ELEMENT

C **8.1.1** Demonstrate suitable preparation (warm-up) of a horse for jumping with regard for weather and ground conditions.

S **8.1.2** Care of the horse after exertion with regard for weather conditions.

What the examiner is looking for

- The warm-up for both the show jumping and cross-country should demonstrate your ability to prepare the horse to jump.

- You should be working in at jumping length and in jumping position (light seat/half seat/poised position).

- Your work should involve transitions, shortening and lengthening (particularly in canter), and perhaps some direct transitions (halt to trot and walk to canter) to demonstrate that the horse is actively in front of your leg. (Element 8.1.1)

- Your work should involve an awareness of ground conditions. If the ground is slippery then you should show judgement of pace, particularly around corners, not making any turns too acute.

- Similarly if it is a cold day and the horse is clipped and feeling a bit full of himself, you should move him around actively to warm him up as soon as possible; whereas on a hot muggy day you may give the horse a break to avoid overstressing him.

- You may be asked about your warm up and you should be able to talk about the preparation in terms of wanting the horse to be warmed up through his muscles, obedient and listening to the aids and in control.

- After any of your jumping sessions you should be sure to allow the horse to get his breath back (especially after cross-country) by walking him around.

- You should also show an awareness of the need to allow the horse to relax, perhaps loosening the girth and dismounting if appropriate.

- In discussion you should be aware of the need to allow a horse to cool down gradually, throwing a sheet over his loins and back, particularly if a cold day, to prevent him from catching a chill.

- You may be asked about when and whether you would wash a horse off after competition and how you would look after him following exertion.

How to become competent

- The warm-up for jumping is vital to the success of the jumping session.

- If the horse is not sufficiently warmed up, loosened up and on the aids then he is more likely to knock show jumps down, run out or refuse both show jumps and cross-country fences.

- Learn to warm up effectively feeling the horse's responsiveness and suppleness, and then learn to use fences progressively, building up in difficulty to develop the horse's confidence and commitment.

- Be able to shorten and lengthen the stride particularly in canter and with regard to cross-country, open the horse up with a short, sharp strong canter or half-speed gallop over a bigger straight distance (50–100 metres/yards).

- Always find out from the horse you are riding, how much 'instant' acceleration he will give you and then how effectively he will come back to you when you ask him to slow down.

- Discuss with anyone you know who competes in eventing how they warm up for show jumping and cross-country and what they do when they have completed those phases.

- Read books about training for competitions, particularly eventing (which covers a show jumping and cross-country phase).

The candidate should be able to:

Ride effectively yet sympathetically over show jumps up to 1m (3ft 3in) while maintaining a balanced, correct and supple seat at all gaits.

ELEMENT

C **9.1.1** Show an effective, positive manner in performance.

C **9.2.1** Show a balanced position from a secure lower leg.

S **9.2.2** Show fluency through the phases of the jump, allowing the horse freedom over the fences.

C **9.3.1** Demonstrate appreciation of rhythm and pace when jumping a course of show jumps.

S **9.4.1** Demonstrate suitable corrections when dealing with refusals or run-outs.

What the examiner is looking for

- Having showed progressive work building up over a grid of three fences you will then be required to jump a course of fences which will include a double (of one or two non-jumping strides).

- You will ride the same horse that you have ridden through the grid work, and the grid should act as a good warm-up so that by now you have developed a rapport with the horse and a feel for how he jumps.

- One at a time, and usually in numerical order, you will jump the course of show jumps, which you should have walked on arrival at the exam centre. (See the suggested course plans, pages 90-91.)

- In jumping the course you must ride a good track, planning your corners and lines of approach and departure to and from each fence. (Element 9.1.1)

- Throughout the course you must sustain a good balanced position, going fluently with the horse and allowing him freedom over the fences. (Elements 9.2.1 and 9.2.2)

- The pace you choose should be appropriate to the horse, the ground conditions and the jumps you are trying to negotiate. (Element 9.3.1)

- You might choose to jump the first fence out of trot (especially if it is still the first part of the grid – which you have been jumping from trot – and it has just been incorporated into the course as the first obstacle). You might also bring the horse back to trot to ride a tight corner if you are on grass and the ground is slippery.

- You would lack judgement of the correct pace if you chose to approach a double of one non-jumping stride (with a distance of 24ft/7.8m) from trot, as the horse would then probably struggle to make the one stride.

- In jumping the course you must show a positive and effective manner, which comes from confidence and competence at this level. (Element 9.1.1)

- You must also be able to deal with minor problems which might arise within the course. If the horse refuses or runs out at a jump, this in itself is not necessarily your fault, but the way in which you deal with the problem will reflect your competence. (Element 9.4.1)

How to become competent

- With regard to the security of your jumping position refer back to earlier advice on improving your position and effect.

- You can only sustain your jumping position and develop its effect and your confidence and competence by plenty of repetition.

- Jumping occasionally, or even once a week, will not convey the competence and therefore confidence that comes from jumping frequently and on several different horses.

- It is possible to improve your jumping position, balance and security by working on the flat in jumping position. Varying your position from sitting to rising, and also standing up in your stirrups so that you learn to find your point of balance over your lower leg, will help strengthen your position. This work should be done in trot and canter so that your jumping position is both flexible and versatile.

- In addition to jumping grids where distances are measured for you and so you know where the horse will take off for each fence, you must also jump plain fences, and courses of fences where you have to link jumps together.

- The fluency of a course is dependent on you being able to maintain the pace through corners and lines of approach, and also in departures, where the horse may lose rhythm as a result of the jump.

- You must learn to judge pace and show the difference between balanced, controlled energy and uncontrolled speed.

- Rhythm and control of pace will enable the horse to jump in a fluent harmonious way, which you should find easier to follow and stay in balance with.

- If the horse is awkward or disobedient and either runs out or refuses at a fence, you must have enough confidence to make a decision about how to correct the horse.

- Learning to make corrections with horses who are awkward about jumping comes from confidence of riding horses who need encouragement or firmness to develop their jumping.

- A well-timed smack with the whip to correct a horse who has been disobedient can be acceptable, but the whip use must be immediately relevant to the fault (e.g. immediately after a refusal and while the horse is still in front of the fence).

- Untimely use of the whip and use of the whip on the neck is rarely helpful in effecting a positive outcome to a fault.

- The more secure your position, and the more horses you have jumped, the more confident you will be in ensuring that any horse goes over a fence if you have directed him at it.

- Confidence develops competence and vice versa.

- Go to jumping competitions and watch how other riders negotiate courses.

- Walk courses so that you are familiar with the way courses develop in difficulty and how corners and changes of rein are built into jumping courses.

- Look at the way jumps are built with fillers to back the horse off or make the jump look more imposing, narrow jumps (stiles) which need more accuracy in riding, and vertical and oxer-type fences.

- If at all possible do some competing yourself, as this always conveys a flair, determination and initiative in your riding that is difficult to achieve from any other source.

- Clear-round jumping at a local venue, Riding Club competitions, unaffiliated classes and then affiliated BSJA classes will all offer something for the developing jumping rider.

The candidate should:

Have knowledge of the rules for riding at competitive and social events.

ELEMENT

S   **10.1.1** Explain the rules for working in at competitive events.

S   **10.2.1** Explain basic principles of welfare for the horse at competitions.

What the examiner is looking for

- This is likely to be examined through questions from the examiner and could be included at any stage during the jumping phase of the exam. It is quite possible that you are not directly aware of it, as it may be covered as part of the discussion about how one or other of the jumping horses went for you.

- You should be able to discuss basic rules for working in at competitive events. These should include checking to see whether you need to declare your intention to compete when you arrive at the competition, wearing the appropriate number for your entry, wearing the designated clothing (e.g. hat with harness/crash helmet and body protector for cross-country), jumping the practice jump the way it is flagged (i.e. red flag on the right, white flag on the left), giving way to other riders, and passing left to left. (Element 10.1.1)

- You should understand the basic principles of the horse's welfare at a competition. (Element 10.2.1)

- The horse should be fit enough to manage the competitive effort being expected of him without stress either during, after or as a result of the competition.

- At the competition you must be aware of the horse's need to be kept warm or cool before competing, depending on the weather.

- Every consideration should be given to ensure the horse cools down and feels comfortable as soon as possible after competing.

- Attention to the horse's need to have water and feed after competing should also be a priority, with due regard for any possible journey home which might also be part of the outing.

How to become competent

- The best way to develop competence in this area is to go to competitions and watch what is done with horses during the warming up and the cooling down after competing.

- Make sure that you go to some top-class events to see how professional riders treat their horses.

- If you can, take the opportunity to learn to groom for a rider at a competition. This is one of the best ways for getting the 'hands on' experience which will give you the closest insight into how horses work and recover after competing.

- Then, if you are able to compete yourself, take the care of your horse very seriously.

- The horse's welfare is a priority and his good health and well-being will ensure that you have plenty of good competitions in the future.

The candidate should be able to:

Ride effectively yet sympathetically over cross-country fences up to 0.91m (3ft), while maintaining a balanced, correct and supple seat at all gaits.

ELEMENT

C   **11.1.1** Show an effective, positive manner in performance.

C   **11.2.1** Show a balanced position from a secure lower leg.

S   **11.2.2** Show fluency through the phases of the jump, allowing the horse freedom over the fences.

C   **11.3.1** Demonstrate appreciation of rhythm and pace when jumping a course of cross-country fences.

C   **11.3.2** Show appreciation of speed with regard for terrain, balance, ground conditions and fence type.

S   **11.4.1** Show appropriate methods of approach for a variety of fence types.

S   **11.5.1** Demonstrate suitable corrections if having to deal with refusals or run-outs.

What the examiner is looking for

- As with the show-jumping phase, the examiner is looking for a purposeful, confident approach so that you ride the horse competently round a simple course of fences. (Element 11.1.1)

- You will have changed horses from your show-jumping ride, but you must still show a secure and balanced position in harmony with the horse. The security of your position must allow you to ride the horse with influence and control, producing a fluent round with an allowing hand over the fences. (Elements 11.2.1 and 11.2.2)

- You must show an understanding of a pace appropriate to cross-country riding, but this will be relevant to the ground conditions (e.g. if the ground is very slippery or hard you might adjust the pace to a slower speed, particularly around corners or turns). It is also important to ride the horse in a good rhythm. (Element 11.3.1)

- The terrain and fence type should also influence your choice of pace (e.g. if jumping down steps or a drop fence, you will need to reduce the pace – while maintaining the power – so that the horse can jump off his hocks and not tip onto the forehand as he lands). You might choose a strong trot or a contained canter rather than a 'forward' canter. (Element 11.3.2)

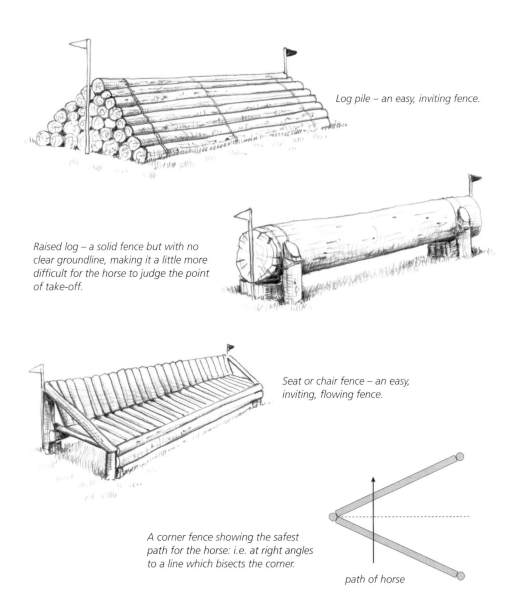

Log pile – an easy, inviting fence.

Raised log – a solid fence but with no clear groundline, making it a little more difficult for the horse to judge the point of take-off.

Seat or chair fence – an easy, inviting, flowing fence.

A corner fence showing the safest path for the horse: i.e. at right angles to a line which bisects the corner.

path of horse

119

- You must show an awareness of how to choose an appropriate approach for a variety of fence types. (Element 11.4.1) Here you should be aware that for angled fences or corners you may still need to choose a straight line at right angles to the fence to allow the horse to jump it with maximum ease).

- You must show some ability to deal with refusals or run-outs in much the same way as was referred to in the previous element. (Element 11.5.1)

How to become competent

- Much of the advice given in the preceding element on show jumping applies here, but with specific reference to cross-country riding.

- Try to attend some good events (British Eventing affiliated competitions) and watch cross-country riding. Especially watch the professional riders and see the fluency and rhythm with which they jump their courses.

- The better the rhythm, the easier it is for the horse to negotiate the jumps.

- Learn to jump cross-country fences from a much stronger canter than you would use for a standard show-jumping round.

- Learn to ride canter easily up and down hills, feeling the balance of the horse and allowing him to use himself up and down gradients.

- Continually consolidate your own balance and position by riding in jumping position frequently (not just when you are jumping).

- Your jumping position will only become really secure and established with much practice.

- Try to take any opportunity to ride cross-country fences, whether in a schooling session, on a cross-country ride with some jumps, or at a one-day event.

Questions and Answers

It is recommended that you obtain a copy of *The BHS Examinations Handbook*. It has a comprehensive list of suggested questions which might be used by examiners during the exam day. Examiners may use the exact wording or adapt the questions to suit the situation, but the knowledge required is the same even if the question is slightly changed.

Below are some of the suggested questions/tasks relating to the Stage 3 syllabus. Some questions are accompanied by a concise, model answer (or answers) indicating an acceptable level of knowledge; others give advice on how to approach answering them. In every case you should try to enhance your answer to show a greater depth of knowledge. A more expansive answer requires that you study each subject a little more deeply, which will enable you to speak with greater confidence when giving your answers.

Structure of the leg below the knee

Q. Using the horse in front of you, show me where you might expect to find a splint.

A. Be able to designate the area where a splint might be present, which is in the region below the knee and anywhere to approximately half way down the cannon bone towards the back of the limb where the splint bones lie.

Splints can be present on the front or hind legs; they may be on the inside or outside of the limb, although they are more commonly found on the inside of the limb.

Q. What could be a possible cause of the horse developing splints, and how are they normally treated?

A. The development of a splint(s) is usually associated with working young horses excessively on hard ground or too much work for the horse whose bone development is still youthful and potentially vulnerable to jarring or over-work.

Splints do, however, occasionally arise through no fault of the horse owner or rider, and can do so in older horses.

Generally the treatment should involve taking the horse out of work, especially while the splint is in the developing stage. The horse may be slightly lame, and the splint may be hot and show some inflammation as it establishes.

Cold hosing will alleviate some heat and discomfort.

Usually splints cause little problem as long as they are not aggravated by hard work during development.

Q. Using the horse in front of you, name the main tendons in the lower leg and show me where they run on the horse.

A. Here you must demonstrate confidence and be able to show directly on the limb where the following tendons run:

- Common digital extensor tendon (front of limb).

- Lateral digital extensor tendon (front of limb).

- Superficial digital flexor tendon (back of limb).

- Deep digital flexor tendon (back of limb).

Q. If a horse strains a tendon what are the likely signs and how is it treated? Can we ever tell if a horse has strained a tendon in the past?

A. The horse is likely to go suddenly lame, or after a hard day's exertion the lower limb (in the tendon region) is likely to swell, show heat and pain on pressure.

The horse should be rested immediately; the vet should be called, as an assessment must be made and the horse may need some pain relief.

Cold hosing is likely to help in relieving the pain, heat and swelling.

The vet should advise on the immediate and longer-term treatment.

Generally, tendon injuries need time for healing.

A limb that has suffered a tendon injury is likely to show some residual damage:

(a) The limb should be cold, but there may be thickening in the tendon region where some rupturing of the tendon sheath or fibres caused scar tissue to develop in the repair of the injury.

(b) The tendon may look 'bowed'.

Q. Show me on the horse in front of you where you would expect to find windgalls. Has the horse got any? Do they need to be treated, and, if so, how?

A. Be sure to know where windgalls occur (small, puffy soft lumps around the fetlock joint, usually on both front or both hind legs – windgalls on a single leg may be a sign of a more serious problem in the affected leg).

Be sure that you can recognise windgalls when they are present.

Usually windgalls do not cause a problem. They are, however, an indication that the horse is subject to a degree of 'wear and tear'.

They become more visible when the ground is hard and the horse is still being asked to compete and work hard.

Take them as a minor warning to keep an eye on how much work you expect of the horse if the ground gets hard.

Q. Using the horse in front of you, show me where the sesamoid bones are. What are their function and what possible problems can occur with them?

A. There are two sesamoid bones in each fetlock joint; they make up part of the fetlock joint in conjunction with the base of the cannon bone and the top of the long pastern bone.

They are smooth, rounded bones over which run some of the tendons on their way to the lower part of the limb and the foot.

The sesamoid bones are vulnerable to knocks from the opposite limb, especially if the horse does not move very well or straight.

The fetlock joint is potentially vulnerable to strain, which may result in inflammation of the sesamoid bones, which is then known as sesamoiditis.

Any bones or joints are susceptible to jarring from excessive work on hard ground.

Q. **What are the main ligaments in the horse's lower leg? Show me where they are on this horse. Are there any problems that can affect them?**

A. Be able to name and designate on the lower limb the following ligaments:

• Superior check ligament (just above the knee).

• Subcarpal check ligament (just below the knee).

• Suspensory ligament.

Ligaments can be damaged in much the same way as tendons, i.e. by pulls and strains (e.g. jumping into heavy ground or when the horse suddenly has to cope with a change of terrain or going).

Ligaments are less elastic and stronger than tendons but once damaged usually need a much longer period of recuperation to recover fully.

The horse's foot

Q. **Assess the balance of the horse's front feet.**

A. Be able to compare the size and shape of both front feet.

Be able to assess the limb alignment or 'column of support' down the limb.

Be able to consider the hoof-pastern axis and whether the weight is distributed evenly over the foot, from front to back and from side to side.

Q. **What problems may be caused by the feet being incorrectly balanced?**

A. The horse may not move fluently, he may pull shoes off.

He may wear his shoes unevenly and eventually he is likely to go lame.

There may be a negative effect on the joints further up the leg.

Q. **Tell me about the hoof-pastern axis of this horse's front feet.**

A. Make sure that you know what the hoof-pastern axis is and how it should appear (the pastern should slope at around 45–50° angle to the ground, and this slope should be in line with the angle of the wall of the hoof).

Be able to describe and recognise, on the horse if necessary, a broken-back hoof-pastern axis and a broken-forward axis.

Q. What problems can arise from an incorrect hoof-pastern axis?

A. A broken-back hoof-pastern axis puts undue strain on the back of the limbs, which might affect the tendons and ligaments in the lower leg.

A broken-forward axis may make the feet more upright and more vulnerable to jarring from concussion.

Q. Look at the wear on this horse's front/hind shoes. What can you tell me about this horse's way of going?

A. Unlevel wear on the shoes will tell you how the horse distributes weight on his feet (even if you cannot see him move).

Be on the look-out for the following:

- Worn toes (does the horse drag his toes?)
- Wear on the outside or inside of the foot or feet – this indicates where the horse takes more pressure on his foot.

Q. Do this horse's feet tell you anything about his general state of health?

A. If the feet are cracked or brittle this may reflect a poor diet.

If the feet show different coloured rings around the horn (not ridges) then this may indicate a period where there was a spurt of horn growth at a time when the horse perhaps had access to different or richer pasture.

Shoeing

Q. Discuss the shoes on the horse in front of you.

A. Be able to look at the front and hind shoes and describe exactly what you see.

Do the shoes look as if they have recently been put on?

Is the foot over-growing the shoe? Are the clenches rising? Are the shoes showing signs of wear?

Q. Where would you find stud holes?

A. Usually they will be visible as small round holes in the heel region of the shoe. They are usually on the outside branch of the shoe and more likely to be found in the hind shoes. Occasionally they may be in the front shoes as well.

Q. How do you clean out stud holes?

A. Pick out the hole with some kind of sharp instrument – a farrier's shoe nail will do the job.

Use a 'T tap' instrument to re-establish the screw threads of the stud hole.

Q. What can you use to plug stud holes?

A. To keep the hole from getting worn out or clogged up with dirt, pack the hole with some greased cotton wool.

Q. What type of studs would you use on hard ground?

A. Sharper, spiked studs will bite into hard ground and give security.

Q. What type of studs would you use on soft ground?

A. Chunky, squarer studs will hold more in heavier ground.

Circulatory system

Q. What does the heart do?

A. The heart acts as the pump for the blood in the body, pushing it around the whole body.

Q. What does the blood take to the various parts of the body?

A. Blood takes oxygen from the lungs to all parts of the body via the heart.

Blood carries water and nutrients from the gut to all parts of the body.

Blood carries hormones from the endocrine glands to other parts of the body.

Blood transports carbon dioxide and waste products from all parts of the body to the lungs and kidneys for disposal.

Q. How would you know if bleeding from a wound was venous or arterial?

A. Venous bleeding is usually less profuse; the blood will be red but not with the same intensity of arterial bleeding.

Arterial bleeding is likely to spurt from the wound (especially if the injury is close to the heart, where the influence of the heart's pumping is greater).

Venous bleeding (from a small or minor vein) will usually stop of its own accord. Arterial bleeding will definitely need veterinary assistance.

Q. How would the type of bleed affect your treatment?

A. If you suspect arterial bleeding you must seek help from a veterinarian and state the urgency of the situation.

Q. Horses' legs often fill when standing in. How is this linked to circulation?

A. When turned out, the horse is constantly on the move. As a browsing animal, it is in his nature to stay quietly on the move for much of his time.

When confined to the stable his natural movement is restricted.

Movement assists in the natural recirculation of blood and lymph up the limbs; the pressure of the foot coming to the ground assists in the blood being pushed back up the leg.

When stabled, this natural assistance is lacking and the blood and lymph tends to accumulate in the lower part of the limbs – hence the condition we know as 'filled legs'.

Q. After exercise a horse's pulse will be raised. What does the time it takes him to recover tell you?

A. The longer it takes for the horse's pulse to return to 'normal' the less fit the horse is and the more the exertion has affected him.

A fit horse will 'recover' much more quickly than an unfit horse.

Respiratory system

Q. Assessing the horse in front of you, what is his respiratory rate at the moment? Explain how you have come to this conclusion.

A. Watch either the rise and fall of his flank, or (if a cold day) watch the exhalation of his breath. A healthy horse will have a respiration rate of between 8 and 12 at rest if nothing is disturbing him.

Q. Identify some of the signs that would indicate respiratory distress and show me on the horse in front of you where you might see these signs.

A. Talk about whistling or roaring and be able to explain why horses suffer from these conditions. Know where the larynx (which these conditions affect) is located..

Whistling and roaring is heard when the horse breathes in.

Know about the Hobday procedure – a minor surgical operation, initiated by a Mr Hobday, to help treat horses with an obstruction to their breathing brought about by damage to the larynx.

Know about 'broken wind' (or emphysema) – a condition which ultimately causes the horse to be starved of air because the lung tissue has lost its elasticity. This reduces the lungs' capability to process oxygen and carbon dioxide efficiently.

Broken wind can sometime be accompanied by a 'heaves line' – a line along the horse's flank which becomes apparent when the horse tightens his muscles in an effort to 'push' out the extra air trapped in the lungs. This line is visible on exhalation.

Q. Show, on the horse in front of you, where the different parts of the respiratory system are located.

A. Be able to show where the nostrils, nasal passage, pharynx, larynx, windpipe, bronchi, bronchioles and alveoli would be in relation to the position of the lungs.

Q. Indicate on the horse in front of you how inhalation and exhalation takes place.

A. Air is breathed in through the nostrils.

It is warmed and filtered (by fine hairs or cilia) in the nasal passage.

It passes over the pharynx and larynx and down the windpipe.

The windpipe branches into two bronchi. (Each lung is supplied by one bronchus.)

The bronchus subdivides in each lung many times, to bronchioles, and ultimately into alveoli or sacs, which is where the exchange of gases takes place.

Oxygen is taken in and carbon dioxide is expelled each time the horse breathes in and out.

Q. What problems might be caused by an allergic reaction in the horse's respiratory tract, and what outward signs will be seen?

A. When a horse develops an allergic reaction to something, he becomes sensitive to it and ultimately may become extremely intolerant to it, his body reacting in an antagonistic way to the apparent foreign body.

He may show some unfamiliar and unexpected symptoms such as intermittent swellings over his body, filled legs or thickening of his glands around the jowl region.

Q. Describe how air passes through the nasal passages and the larynx, showing the location of the different organs on the horse in front of you.

A. Make sure you know where the parts of the respiratory system are on the horse.

See the answers to the similar question above.

Q. What problems may be caused to a horse's respiration by a full stomach?

A. The horse's stomach lies in close proximity to his lungs – the abdominal cavity (where the stomach is situated) being separated from the thorax (chest cavity where the lungs lie) by the diaphragm – and if the stomach is full and the horse has to work hard, the amount of room that his lungs have to expand is restricted. The efficient functioning of the diaphragm will also be restricted.

The horse may suffer digestive problems because the food cannot be digested properly because the lungs are making demands on oxygen.

Similarly the lungs may not get sufficient air for the work required if a full stomach restricts the space for expansion of the lung tissue.

Q. What aspects of either the environment of his stable or outside in the stable yard could cause this horse's respiratory rate to change?

A. Consider all the circumstances around you which might affect the horse: e.g. sources of sudden noises that might disturb him; horses coming and going, which could affect the quietness in the yard; vehicles which might start up and move about. His respiratory rate could also be affected by a dusty environment, or if he is too hot (wearing too much clothing) and/or if his stable is poorly ventilated.

Conformation

Practical oral

The following questions may be asked of you in the Practical Oral section. Make sure that you have practised looking at many different horses and you can assess them systematically and describe what you see.

Q. Assessing the horse in front of you, do you consider him to be 'in proportion'?

Q. What problems in his conformation do you consider may affect his performance?

Q. How will his conformation affect his movement?

Q. When assessing the horse in front of you, what factors might affect his soundness for the work?

Q. In looking at the forelimb of this horse, do you consider the limb less than ideal or do you consider that the horse has a good forelimb? Please discuss.

Q. The horse's hocks are sometimes described as bow-legged, cow-hocked or sickle-hocked – please describe this horse's hocks.

Ailments/care of sick and lame horses

Practical oral

Q. Where on this horse would you find a girth gall? How would you treat it and how could you prevent it in the future?

A. It would be visible as a nick or bare patch of skin in the fold of skin around the area where the girth lies immediately behind the elbow.

If it is sore and the skin is red and angry then bathe first to soothe the region. If the skin is not broken then saline solution could help to harden the area.

Use a soft sheepskin type sleeve over the girth or work the horse without a saddle until the area is no longer red.

In future, use saline solution to harden the area prior to the horse coming back into work if he has been in soft condition with little work. Use a soft, clean girth and take care with the careful fitting of any type of girth or roller to prevent galling.

Q. What does ringworm look like and where on the horse does it usually occur? What action would you take?

A. Round areas of raised hair (prior to the hair falling out) or pink or grey patches about the size of a 50 pence piece.

Patches may be visible anywhere on the body, but are often found on the neck, shoulders, and face.

Immediately isolate the horse and monitor other horses that may have been in contact with the infected horse. Follow the isolation procedure strictly.

Consult the vet for the most appropriate treatment (usually an oral medication). It is often necessary to treat more than one horse in the yard to avoid a spread.

Take the vet's advice on washing the horse in an antifungal wash.

Q. If this horse had laminitis, what symptoms would he be presenting? How would you treat this problem and how could it be prevented in the future?

A. He would be extremely uncomfortable on his feet, attempting to alleviate the weight on his feet; he may draw his hind legs well under the body or tip onto the heels of his front feet.

The feet would feel hot and the horse would be very lame and reluctant to move.

Call the vet who would advise on the most up-to-date treatment according to what had been the cause for that horse.

Antihistamine injections may be used, as would some kind of pain relief.

If incorrect feeding has been the cause then this must be addressed for the future.

It is important not to allow animals to become overweight, especially in the spring, and ponies may need to have restricted access to any spring grass.

Q. You visit this horse in the morning and notice that he has a nasal discharge, runny eyes and looks listless. What action do you take?

A. Take his temperature (should be around 100.5 °F or 38 °C).

Offer him clean fresh water and some food to see how interested he is in eating.

Monitor him over the next few hours, but consider calling the vet if there is no improvement in him or if he has a temperature of more than one or two degrees above normal.

Keep him quiet and isolated from other horses. Make sure he is warm enough and has a good deep bed with a plentiful supply of fresh clean water. Monitor him constantly. Keep him comfortable, with his eyes and nose bathed to keep them clean.

Q. This horse has suspected colic. What are some of the signs of colic and how would you treat the horse?

A. The horse is restless and showing discomfort. He may paw the ground, kick at his stomach, look at his stomach, and get up and down in an effort to find a comfortable stance. He may at worst become violent, throwing himself around in pain.

Immediately call the vet. Colic can be very serious and the sooner it is treated, the better.

Remove the water bucket and any other moveable stable fittings. Bed down with extra bedding (if this can be done safely).

Monitor the horse constantly. If he is only mildly uncomfortable and it is a warm day, it can help to turn him out in a small paddock.

When the vet arrives, be able to tell him exactly what has happened to the horse in the previous 24 hours.

Treat the horse as per the vet's instructions and then give him good nursing care after his colic for 12 to 24 hours, or longer if he has been very ill.

Q. The horse had a fall while jumping. Upon investigation of his limbs you notice a swelling appearing on the back of one of his forelegs, between the knee and the fetlock. What do you suspect has occurred? How would you deal with this?

A. It is likely that the horse has damaged a tendon in the region between the knee and fetlock.

Immediate treatment would be to apply cold water (usually hosing the limb is easiest – for 15 to 20 minutes at a time, three or four times a day).

It would be wise to consult the vet for professional advice on how bad the damage might be and what the best treatment is.

Tendon injuries always benefit from long periods of recuperation to allow the damage to repair itself, but the vet can advise on anti-inflammatory and pain-relieving drugs, which might help in the acute stage.

Q. What is a curb? Where on the horse would you find one? How does it occur and how should it be treated?

A. A curb is a strain to the ligament at the back of the hock, resulting in a thickening which is seen as a convex soft bulge on the back of the hock just below the point of the hock.

It occurs as a result of strain, sometimes with young horses working in soft and holding ground.

Some horses may be more prone to curbs if their hocks are rather weak or sickle shaped, which puts more strain onto the area where a curb would arise.

Usually they cause little or no concern other than a visual blemish. If there is any heat or pain while the curb is developing then it is wise to cold hose the area and rest the horse until any initial inflammation has gone.

Q. It is spring. The horse has been diagnosed as being infested with lice. Where on the horse do you normally find lice? How do you treat this problem?

A. Lice are usually found in the horse's mane and tail but may spread over the whole body if the infestation is allowed to proceed untreated.

Consult the vet for the appropriate treatment; he will advise on what is current and permissible.

Treatment will probably require two or three repetitions to ensure that the eggs are 'caught' as they hatch. Ten-day intervals between treatments are usually appropriate.

Q. What symptoms other than a cough lead you to diagnose broken wind or COPD? What could you do to alleviate the situation?

A. The horse struggles to work efficiently, showing signs of breathlessness and fatigue in spite of being fit enough for his work.

There may be a 'heave line' along the lower edge of his ribs, where he employs his abdominal muscles in a double exhale to try to push the stale air out of his lungs because the alveoli have lost elasticity and function.

Keep the horse as slim as possible and keep him fit.

Work him outside as much as possible and if possible keep him in an outside stable rather than an American barn type.

Feed him damp feed and haylage to avoid any dust allergies or implications from dry food.

Turn him out as much as possible.

Use dust-free bedding in his stable

Theory section

Q. Your horse has a fever. List the principles of sick nursing.

A. Isolate from other horses.

Warm stable with a deep bed and light warm clothing, bandages if necessary.

Ready supply of fresh water, with the chill taken off if necessary.

One person only to look after the horse to be able to monitor his well-being and to keep the risk of cross-infection to a minimum.

Small feeds of a succulent and palatable nature; reduce all hard feed and keep the horse on a laxative high-fibre ration.

Administer any medication prescribed by the vet, with a record kept of what was given, by whom, and when.

Peace and quiet for the horse but plenty of TLC.

Q. You are starting up a yard and need to stock an equine medicine cabinet. List some items you would include.

A. • A safe, clearly marked lockable cabinet or cupboard that has the vet's telephone number and any relevant emergency numbers clearly listed on the door or inside.

• A small variety of sterile dressings and bandages for emergency use.

• Thermometer.

• Small bowl (for treating wounds with saline solution).

• Salt (if not in the feed room).

• Blunt-ended scissors.

• Gamgee tissue, cotton wool or similar material for swabs.

• Some type of wound dressing (powder or cream).

• Simple eye ointment (for runny eyes from flies).

- Perhaps worm doses.

- Perhaps a stethoscope.

- Perhaps a twitch.

Q. Discuss some points that indicate good health/poor health in the horse.

A. Good health:

- Bright eyes, no discharge.

- Horse is alert, interested in surroundings, eating, drinking normally.

- Taking weight evenly on all four limbs.

- Horse looks at ease with himself.

- Coat glossy and flexible.

- Passing droppings and urine easily and regularly.

Poor health:

- A harsh, 'starey' coat.

- A horse that is thin and does not maintain weight in spite of appearing to eat well may be in poor health.

- A horse with a 'pot' belly may be suffering from a worm infestation.

Q. What is a poultice/tubbing/fomenting? What type of ailments would you use these treatments for? How would you apply them?

A. A **poultice** is used for drawing out heat or infection from a wounded area. It is made from a substance that holds the heat well (e.g. bran or kaolin) or can be a custom-made preparation such as Animalintex.

It can be used on any site where it can be attached, but is most effectively used on the feet or limbs.

Tubbing is used for the feet and can be carried out with hot or cold water, depending on the treatment. Hot tubbing would be to draw (similar to a poultice); cold tubbing would be to reduce heat and inflammation.

The heels should always be greased prior to tubbing to avoid any soreness arising from the heel region becoming water-logged.

Fomenting is a term used for applying heat or cold to an area. Sustained heat or cold is applied for a 15–20 minute period to promote circulation and blood flow, which in turn aids in the healing process.

Q. How do you take the temperature/pulse/respiration of a horse? What readings would you expect in a healthy horse?

A. Respiration is taken by counting the horse's inhalations and exhalations (breathing in and out); there should be around 8 to 12 breaths per minute in a healthy horse at rest.

Watch the horse's flank rising and falling; or in winter watch the horse's out-breaths, which will be visible in the cold.

The pulse rate is taken by feeling the horse's submaxillary artery where it crosses over the jaw bone (under the jowl). Feel the pulse with your index and second fingers. Count for 30 seconds and double it.

A healthy horse's pulse will be around 36–42 beats per minute at rest.

The temperature is taken by inserting a thermometer into the side of the horse's anus. Grease the thermometer and make sure someone holds the horse if it is likely to be anxious.

The thermometer should be read after one minute. In a healthy horse at rest it should be 37.8–38.3 °C or 100–101 °F.

Q. Discuss the four main types of wound that can afflict the horse. How would you treat them?

A. The four main categories of wound are:

Bruised or contused wounds – No outward break to the skin; internal rupture of blood vessels, causing discoloration or bruising, heat and pain on pressure; the horse may be in pain although the cause may not be immediately visible. Caused by a blow with a blunt object – commonest cause: a kick.

Clean cut/incised wounds – Easy to stitch, as such cuts have clean edges with minimal trauma; often minimal bleeding for the same reason; should heal easily as long as kept clean. Glass and metal cause incised wounds.

Torn or lacerated wounds – Characterised by tearing, with trauma, as cause is due to something rough, e.g. barbed wire; messy wounds, with edges not easily drawn together; often a lot of blood from torn blood vessels and much pain due to damage to nerve endings.

Puncture wounds – Characterised by deep penetration with only a small entry hole; easily infected due to healing on top with debris or infection still within the body. Nails, thorns etc. typically cause puncture wounds.

Treatment of wounds in general requires skill, veterinary advice in any other than the simplest of cases and certainly if a joint, profuse bleeding or trauma is involved.

General rules for wound treatment would include stopping the bleeding, cleanliness, access to open air to aid healing, and attention to anti-tetanus protection.

Q. Your horse becomes cast in the stable. What does this mean, how does it occur and what action will be taken?

A. A horse gets cast in his stable when he has lain down in such a position that he has got stuck against a wall and is unable to gain sufficient purchase with his legs to enable him to stand up.

You may find him upside down on his back with his legs stuck against the wall.

You will need help and some sturdy rope.

One person reassures the horse at his head, in a kneeling position, keeping the horse's neck still and his head on the floor.

The second person wraps the rope loosely around the hind and front legs of the two legs furthest away from you (against the wall). The horse is then pulled gently over, using the ropes.

The timing is crucial. As the horse feels himself come free, he will struggle to get up. Both people should quickly move away from the horse on the same side.

Q. When would you isolate a horse? What procedures do you follow when isolating a horse?

A. You may isolate a horse when he first comes to a new yard to ensure that he does not transfer anything (e.g. a contagious condition) he may have brought with him.

Isolation would also be appropriate for a horse that develops a condition that you do not want to spread to the rest of the yard (e.g. ringworm).

Isolation procedure involves:

- Placing the horse in a stable away from any other horses (but still so that he can see something going on in the yard).

- One person only to look after the horse.

- Separate equipment (feed utensils, grooming kit, mucking-out tools, etc.) for the horse.

- A record kept of treatment.

- Bedding, uneaten feed, dressings, etc. burnt if possible to avoid infection.

- The stable should be disinfected after the horse has recovered and all bedding burnt.

- All rugs, tack, grooming kit, etc. disinfected, washed or cleaned thoroughly.

Horse Behaviour

The horse at grass

Q. What 'vices' make it dangerous to run a particular horse with a large group?

A. Biting or kicking or bullying.

Q. What characteristics make it dangerous to turn out a particular horse with a group of horses?

A. If a horse has strong male characteristics (in spite of being a gelding), he may 'herd' the other horses, especially if there are mares and geldings together, and he may fight with the geldings.

Q. What problems of behaviour can occur when mares are in season and running with geldings?

A. The geldings may become territorial and try to assert themselves as head of the herd.

Q. Do young horses and older horses run well together? How might the youngsters' behaviour annoy or upset the older horses?

A. It can work, but sometimes the youngsters will run around to amuse themselves and disturb the older horses, who are not interested in 'playing'.

It is important to assess each group and their behaviour and make changes if some horses are not settling and others are being disturbed.

The horse when stabled

Q. What stable vices would you watch for?

A. You could see weaving, crib biting, windsucking, box walking, tearing rugs, kicking, and banging the door.

Q. The new horse is standing in his stable swaying from side to side. (a) What is this called? (b) What would you do about it?

A. (a) Weaving.

(b) Try to make sure that the horse spends time out of his stable more than once a day; try to turn him out or exercise him on a horse walker if available; give him ad lib hay or something to 'play' with to occupy him; keep him in a part of the yard where he has plenty to look at to try to wean him from his habit.

Q. The new horse in the yard is described as being quiet in the stable and having no vices. What sort of behaviour would make you think he was wrongly described?

A. He appears agitated and unsettled, he may be pacing around the stable or banging the door.

He might exhibit a tendency to weave.

He is difficult to catch when you go into the stable; he does not come to you but turns his back to you and hides his face in the corner.

Q. What causes a horse to:
   (a) weave?
   (b) crib bite?
   (c) windsuck?

A. In general, these vices can be picked up from seeing another horse behave this way; and there is some evidence that a horse can have a predisposition towards one or more of these vices from his gene pool.

A horse that is bored and confined to his stable for long periods is more likely to develop a vice than a happy, well-occupied one.

Q. The new horse is very nervous of people and is difficult to handle. How can you gain his confidence?

A. Put the horse next to a calm, confident horse who will give the anxious horse more security.

Appoint a competent, calm, positive person to look after the nervous horse to give him more confidence through the way he is handled.

Ensure a regular daily routine.

The horse when ridden

Q. Jogging is a bad habit. What can it be a sign of?

A. Anxiety on the part of the horse (or rider), bad training, or being 'fresh'.

Q. Your horse persistently refuses a jump he has been over before. What can he be trying to tell you?

A. The horse is telling you that although he has jumped the jump before, it was not a good experience for him and he has no intention of repeating it again:

- perhaps the jump had something to fear that he had not anticipated (a ditch on the landing side, water underneath, etc.), or

- the rider gave the horse a bad experience over the fence (jabbed him in the mouth, or sat heavily on his back), or

- he has repeatedly jumped this fence and is bored, or

- the tack may have hurt him in some way as he jumped.

Q. Bad management – overfeeding and underworking – may cause the horse to behave badly when ridden. In what way may this be shown?

A. If the horse is overfed and underworked, he is likely to be explosive and unreasonable to ride. He may buck, try to run away and generally be tense, sharp and unruly in his behaviour.

He may be so tense that he is bad-tempered with other horses, trying to bite or kick.

Q. What is meant when a horse is said to be 'nappy'? How does he behave and what are some of the possible causes?

A. A nappy horse will try not to leave his stable or his 'friends'; he will be reluctant to work independently and confidently on his own, taking any opportunity to try to take the rider home.

The horse may be nappy through inadequate training or riding – he has been allowed to 'do what he likes'. Leaving other horses has not been enforced and he thinks he can stay 'in the herd'.

He may be nappy through fear or lack of confidence in his rider.

Q. An older horse who normally jumps well begins to jump badly. What might he be trying to tell you?

A. He may have some pain or discomfort in part of his anatomy (teeth or back).

His tack may be causing him some discomfort.

His training may not be correct and he has lost confidence.

Q. What changes in behaviour might signify to you that the horse is uncomfortable, unwell or physically stressed?

A. Reluctance to go forward when he is normally easily forward.

Any change in the horse's 'normal' behaviour which is unaccountable.

Any change in the horse's eating habits or any underlying change in the appearance of the horse.

Any obvious sign of unlevelness in gait or non-acceptance of the tack being applied.

Q. A young horse starts rushing his fences. What is he trying to tell you?

A. The horse is indicating a lack of confidence in his training and starting to rush 'to get it over with as soon as possible'.

He might also be indicating an over-confidence in what he is learning.

Q. How can a nervous rider affect a horse's behaviour?

A. Horses are followers generally, not leaders; they need to take confidence from their rider, and if they are ridden by a nervous rider then a downward spiral can develop. The horse becomes less confident as the rider lacks the competence to develop the horse.

Care of the competition horse (as a groom)

Q. What health checks would you make to a competition horse on a regular basis?

A. General appearance; eating well; drinking; droppings/urine normal.

Temperature, pulse and respiration.

Thorough check of legs and feet when grooming daily.

Q. What checks concerning the horse's tack, shoeing, travelling arrangements and equipment, would you make prior to competitions?

A. If competing regularly then a consistent programme for checking everything would evolve. Until this is well established then a list would be helpful to avoid anything being overlooked.

Make sure shoeing is consistent and new shoes are not fitted in the last few days before a competition.

Make sure all tack is regularly maintained, checked and cleaned. All competition tack should be listed and checked into the lorry.

Make sure all requirements in the way of feed, water, forage and veterinary (first aid) necessities are listed and accounted for.

Make sure that the vehicle used for travelling is roadworthy, safe for the horse and has sufficient fuel.

Q. What preparations would you make on the day before the competition?

A. Ensure the lorry has fuel, oil and water; also check the tyres.

Make sure that all equipment was accounted for and loaded into the lorry.

Check the time of departure and make sure that the route to the competition is known and if necessary written down.

Make sure the lorry is clean, and a haynet tied ready for loading (if necessary).

Assemble all travel equipment the night before and have ready any grooming kit/plaiting equipment that will be needed in the morning.

Q. What actions do you take on the day of competition to keep stress to the horse to a minimum? Consider the various weather conditions that may prevail.

A. The more organised you are and the more 'normal' you keep the competition day, the more likely you are to minimise stress.

If everything is well prepared in advance then it should be easy to keep the day itself calm.

It may be necessary to have an earlier start than usual but, even so, the horse should be fed and his normal routine kept as near the same as possible, apart from the earlier start.

The more calm and relaxed you are, the less the horse is likely to get excited by the change of 'atmosphere'.

If the weather is inclement then you must use your judgement as to the clothing the horse will travel in. He should not travel in clothing that is too heavy or does not 'breathe'. Since he is likely to get hotter while travelling, and as long as the ventilation is good, he may be more comfortable in lighter 'wickable' type rugs for the journey.

Q. What checks and care would you carry out:

(a) On return from a competition?

A. Make sure the horse is cool and has travelled home well.

Check his legs for any signs of injury or fatigue.

Look at his overall well-being (is he tired? off his food? any other signs of abnormality?).

Have you made every provision for his comfort?

(b) On the day following a competition (consider stress, both mental and physical)?

A. Has he eaten and drunk overnight? Has he functioned normally (droppings/urine)?

Are his legs cold and clean?

Is he glad to greet you even though he may be tired?

He should be allowed an 'easy' day, either being led out for grass, or better still, turned out for an hour or two.

He should have his legs and feet thoroughly checked for any problems.

Always trot him up to check soundness.

(c) During the few days following a competition?

A. He should be checked for any signs of injury and lameness which may erupt a few days after the competition (e.g. a puncture wound in the foot).

Always monitor the work, the competition and the way in which the horse recovers after the competition. This will help to ensure that you are providing a well-balanced plan for the build-up to the competition, the day itself and the days after the exertion.

Taking the Exam

You should, by now, be developing a more confident approach to your exams and be familiar with the protocol of BHS examinations.

Exam psychology

- Remember to exude confidence and show the examiners your competence.

- Remind yourself throughout the day that you are well prepared and have both the knowledge and practical experience to satisfy the examiners that you are well up to the standard required.

- Continually remind yourself that nothing you will be asked to do or talk about will come as a surprise to you, because your Stage 3 knowledge and practice are sound.

- If something unexpected happens or a question is phrased in an unfamiliar way, deal with it as you would at home. If you are not sure what information is being sought, ask for clarification.

- React and deal with situations in a practical, confident way, leaving the examiner with the feeling that you would be capable of coping with minor crises if they arose in your work situation.

What to wear

Turn-out for the day must be neat, workmanlike and professional. As in any of the exams that you have already sat (BHS or Pony Club), you should wear beige or fawn breeches; with clean leather boots, or short boots and leather half chaps, or a clean pair of rubber riding boots. A shirt and tie or stock with a tweed jacket completes the outfit.

Do wear gloves, and make sure your hair is neat and tidy (tied back or in a hairnet). Take an extra waistcoat or sweater if you want to take off your jacket during the stable management section.

Make sure you have a short and a long whip, and a body protector for the cross-country phase.

TYPICAL EXAMINATION DAY TIMETABLE

3 examiners, including 1 chief
10 RIDING candidates
12 CARE candidates

8.00 - 8.15	Candidates assemble	
8.15	Riding candidates walk jumping courses	
8.30	Candidates introduction and briefing	
9.00	1 to 5	Riding on the flat
	7 to 12	Practical stable management
10.00	7 to 11	Riding on the flat
	1 to 6	Practical stable management
11.00	BREAK	
11.10	1 to 5	Jump riding - show jump then cross country
	7 to 12	Theory
12.10	7 to 11	Jump riding - show jump then cross country
	1 to 6	Theory
1.10	LUNCH	
2.00	1 to 6	Lungeing
	7 to 12	Practical oral
3.10	7 to 12	Lungeing
	1 to 6	Practical oral
4.20	EXAM ENDS	

You will be given a sticky label on which to write your name. Use the name that you are familiar with being called, but make sure that the chief examiner has your name spelt correctly on the list that will be used to fill in your certificate when you achieve it.

Exam procedure

- The exam will take all day (see sample timetable above). Usually the riding and jumping take place in the morning, being run concurrently with some of the stable management sections.

- The stable management is split into three sections (as in Stage 2), namely: practical, practical oral, and theory. You should be able to see from the text of the syllabus what is examined in each section.

- In the riding sections there will be a maximum of five candidates in each group; in the stable management there will be up to six in each group.

- Be polite to other members of your group(s) but avoid being influenced by them. Do not be drawn into conversations about particular horses used in the exam, whether ridden or used in the stable management tests. For example, avoid listening to observations which may go like this: 'The bay horse I rode is awful in canter; it won't go on the left lead and it stops if you have to show jump it.' Or: 'The grey horse in the third stable on the left has a splint on the near-fore, or actually I think it might be on the off-fore.' Information like this is wholly unhelpful and may affect your ability to assess the horse in a completely independent way.

- Make sure that you are focused throughout the day, demonstrating your competence in every section.

- Stay warm and dry, and take a packed lunch and plenty of water to drink. Drink water regularly through the day – it helps to keep you alert and concentrating.

- Make sure that you have some sturdy shoes or Wellingtons to wear when you walk the cross-country fences (and show jumps if on wet grass) so that you keep your riding boots clean for the ridden sections of the exam.

- Make sure that you wear gloves for the riding and lungeing and that you have your gloves and hat available for the trotting up in hand and loading sections of the exam.

- Take a change of clothes with you so that if you get wet during the day you can change to drive home. You do not want to tackle a long journey home in wet clothing.

- At the end of the day give your arm numbers to the examiner who takes you for the last section, and make sure you collect all your belongings. You should receive your results by post in around five to ten days.

Further Reading

The following books and booklets can all be obtained from the BHS Bookshop.

The BHS Complete Manual
of Stable Management

The BHS Veterinary Manual

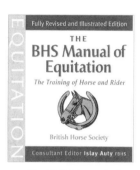

The BHS Manual of
Equitation

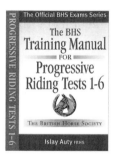

The BHS Training Manual for
Progressive Riding Tests 1-6

The BHS Training
Manual for Stage 1

The BHS Training
Manual for Stage 2

The BHS Training
Manual for the PTT

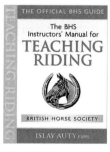

The BHS Instructors'
Manual for Teaching
Riding

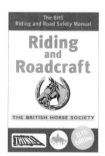

The BHS Riding and
Road Safety Manual –
Riding and Roadcraft

Guide to BHS Examinations

Examinations Handbook

BHS Guide to Careers with Horses

Duty of Care

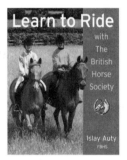

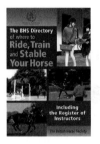

Learn to Ride with The British Horse Society

The BHS Directory of Where to Ride, Train and Stable your Horse